Contents

The ever present

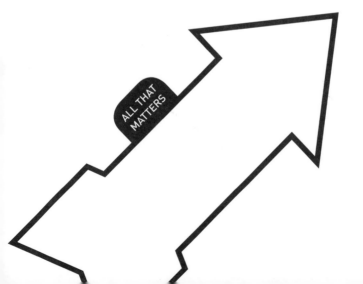

FUTURE

Ziauddin Sardar

7000409234C9

First published in Great Britain in 2013 by Hodder & Stoughton. An Hachette UK company.

First published in US in 2013 by The McGraw-Hill Companies, Inc.

This edition published 2013

Typeset by Cenveo® Publisher Services.

Printed and bound in Great Britain by CPI Group (UK) Ltd., Croydon, CRO 4YY.

Hodder & Stoughton policy is to use papers that are natural, renewable and recyclable products and made from wood grown in sustainable forests. The logging and manufacturing processes are expected to conform to the environmental regulations of the country of origin.

Hodder & Stoughton Ltd

338 Euston Road

London NW1 3BH

www.hodder.co.uk

Also available in ebook

So, what are you doing tomorrow?

Assuming that it is an ordinary working day, and you are fortunate enough to have a job, tomorrow should be like yesterday. The alarm will wake you up at an appointed time, you will pay the obligatory visit to the bathroom, have your breakfast and set off to work. But just because everything was as it ought to be yesterday, it does not mean that tomorrow will be exactly the same. There could be problems with transport or the weather which would change the course of the day. There could be even worse scenarios: a family problem forces you to change your routine, you could be involved in an accident or turn up at the office to discover you have been sacked or made redundant. There are, of course, positive scenarios too. Everything flows as it should, you end up being promoted, receive even better news and end up at a celebratory dinner. But you cannot know for sure. Unlike yesterday, about which you know certain facts, there is uncertainty about tomorrow: almost anything unexpected can happen.

There is another odd thing about tomorrow, well illustrated by the title of a Bond film: *Tomorrow Never Dies* (1997). It is always the day after today, forever alive, pregnant with both positive and negative possibilities. We often use tomorrow to refer to, as *The Concise Oxford Dictionary* puts it, 'some future time'. Like tomorrow, the future, an amalgam of all our tomorrows, is always over the horizon, permanently in front of us. It never comes, and in this sense it is not 'real' and does not really 'exist'. The future can only exist when it becomes the present – but at that point it ceases to be the future. It can never be grasped fully and is permanently unknown.

That is probably why most people do not spend much time thinking about the future. Most of our concerns are focused on the present which has enough issues of its own. We may think about what we are going to do tomorrow or next week, look forward to things that are definite such as birthdays, holidays or religious festivals, and worry about taxes and the education of our children. But we feel helpless about our long-term future. Unlike the past, which we can 'see' as it has left evidence that can be observed and studied, there is nothing to see about the future, there is no evidence we can examine or experience to which we can relate. It is as though we are moving from the brightness of the day to the darkness of the night. Given how rapidly society is changing, how uncertain it all appears, it seems unrealistic to think about the long-term future, even in personal terms. The future appears a remote, vague concept somewhere ahead in time. We are thus inclined to throw our hands in the air and paraphrase Matthew 6:34: the future will take care of itself.

If only. The future does not always take care of itself. Think about it in personal terms. You know you are going to get old and will have to make plans for a comfortable old age. If you are a young person, old age may be 30 or even 40 years in the future. But unless you set up a pension now, and it has ample time to mature, you will not have a pension and may spend your senior years in penury. If you decide to have children you will commit yourself to decades in the future: a baby is not just a baby, it is also an infant, a teenager, a juvenile, a young adult; and it is not just the pram and childcare you need to worry about but also schools and higher education, the difficulties of adolescence, tears and tantrums as well as the joys of achievements and marriage. You know you are going to die one day – that is a future fact – and if you do not want to leave your affairs in a mess you ought to have a will, written, witnessed, signed and sealed in good time. So even in our personal lives we need to do certain things in the present to ensure certain outcomes, despite all the uncertainties, in the future. Thus, the future does not just happen by itself, automatically. It is created through our actions or inaction in the present.

Even though the future does not exist at present, except as an image in our minds, it is something quite real. Unlike Han Solo of *Star Wars*, Captain James T. Kirk of *Star Trek* and the *Terminator*, which are figments of imagination, the future is real and will be realized in tangible form one day. And the form the future will take has a direct and intimate relationship both with our present and our past. We use the experience of the past, its memories, lessons, successes and setbacks, to make decisions and choices in the present. What we do in the present – the desires we have, the perceptions we inculcate, the choices we make, the actions we take – all shape our future. The present thus has a shifting boundary between what has happened and what will happen. The future is ever present in the present.

Moreover, not everything that will happen in the future is unknown to us. There are certain aspects of the future we know quite well. We can, for example, calculate celestial movements with stunning accuracy. That is why we are able to land a man on the moon, send probes to Mars and

Jupiter, and predict solar and lunar eclipses centuries in advance. Meteorologists can provide us with a reasonably confident forecast (although there are always gremlins in the system) of what the weather will be like tomorrow, next week and even a month or two ahead. As individuals we know that we are going to grow old and die one day. We know that a decade or two from now society will definitely change, although we do not know exactly how it will change. We know that climate change or some other environmental catastrophe will have dire consequences for the future of the planet even though we may not know what to do about it. So there are certain aspects of the future we do know about. But on the whole, we can say, after eighteenth-century French mathematician and astronomer Pierre-Simon Laplace, 'What we know is not much. What we do not know is immense.'

An adventure is coming up.

▲ Futures are full of potentials and possibilities.

The paradoxical characteristics of the future – it does not exist but it is real, it is ahead but also behind us, it never arrives but is always with us, it is unknowable yet there are things we do know – make it unique, allusive and a very important subject of study. One way or another, what happens in the future will affect us all. As such, every single person on the planet has an investment in the future; it is a subject that should concern us all. Particularly so in a rapidly changing world, where people's values, attitudes and beliefs change almost as swiftly as new inventions and innovations are produced. By thinking creatively about the future – what might happen, what we would like to happen, what we would have to do to ensure that certain things happen – we, as individuals and communities, can prepare for tomorrow and make more rational decisions on the kind of future we desire and make an effort to achieve it.

What the study of the future is not about

Exploring the future is not about astrology, horoscopes, religious prophecy and the like. Consult the astrology page of popular press, Mystic Meg and Nostradamus for these.

It is also not about futures markets, futures exchanges, futures trading and futures contracts; the stuff of financial meltdowns and nightmares. It has nothing to do with futurism, which is an early twentieth-century art movement, associated with Italian fascists.

'Our civilisation,' writes the American futurist Allen Tough, 'has enormous potential not only to flourish happily but also to deteriorate appallingly. In fact, humanity literally has the capacity to exterminate itself, thus joining many other species that have become extinct. However, our civilisation also has the capacity to avoid the worst dangers and to flourish peacefully for thousands of years. At this peculiar moment in human history, our two extreme potentials (for destroying everything and for achieving a highly positive future) may both be vaster than at any time during the past 10,000 years.'[1] What will actually happen, to our civilization, our communities and societies, depends on the choices we make and the actions we take in the coming years and decades. Change is inevitable, but all of us have to participate in ensuring that change is constructive.

▶ Inquiry not discipline

But how do we study a subject that is so imperceptible, real but absent, that forces us to look backwards (in recent history) as well as forwards? The study of the future may appear, at first sight, to be quite daunting and problematic. But in many respects it is not all that different from other disciplines such as art, music, law, ethics, philosophy and religion, that deal with abstract ideas and phenomena that cannot be measured precisely. Just because the future has some perplexing characteristics, it does not mean we cannot study it in a disciplined, systematic manner, or conduct empirical research on trends and agents of change, or analyse critically the underlying assumptions about our perceptions, metaphors and images of the time ahead – just like any other discipline.

But unlike most established disciplines, such as biology, economics or sociology, the study of the future does not have fixed boundaries, theories, paradigms, authorities and well-established designated areas of research and thought. So it would be wrong to think of it as a discipline.

Rather, the study of the future is a systematic but open-ended mode of inquiry. On the whole, what we actually study when we study the future is the ideas – yours, mine, theirs – about what society, world, humanity and planet will be like in the decades to come. As your ideas about the future are as important and valid as mine, and those of others, the future, and its exploration, becomes an area that is constantly and continuously negotiated and contested. Moreover, we cannot really study 'the future' in the abstract; we have to be explicit and talk about the future of something specific – an object, subject or situation – and then examine how it will change, develop and look in the decades to come. So we may, for example, look at the future of the internet, education, pensions, genetic technology, farming, water, climate and the Middle East. The subject on which we focus will of course have its own disciplinary requirements. We have to know something about economics or the politics of the Middle East before we can look at their future. Thus, the study of the future is, by definition, a multidisciplinary and transdisciplinary endeavour.

When most people think about the future they tend to think, almost by a reflex action, about predictions. This is partly due to the fact that historically the future has been associated with astrology, prophecy, crystal gazing and other arcane forms of divination and supernatural practices. And partly due to the fact that popular literature about the future is essentially about predictions. However, while any enterprise about the future would involve an attempt or two to *predict the future* based on extrapolation from present-day trends, predictions are only a small part of the story. Thinking more constructively about, as well as anticipating, the future requires us to go beyond predictions, not least because predictions are a hazardous business. In most cases, predictions and forecasts simply end up by projecting the (selected) past and the (often-privileged) present on to a linear future. A good example is provided in an article on 'green predictions' in the United Airlines in-flight magazine, *Hemispheres*, which I came across during a jaunt across the United States. 'In the future,' it stated confidently, 'here's how it is going to work: sidewalks will power streetlights, buildings will eat smog, nuclear plants will run on nuclear waste, and endangered animals will be socially networked.'[2]

These predictions tell us nothing more than what technology is being developed at the moment, with added wishful thinking about their dissipation in society in the next few years. Of course, some of these developments will go by the wayside, others will face manufacturing problems, and still others (like the wonderful nuclear plant) will be resisted by pressure groups. Notice also that all of these predictions are about technology, which is usually the case with most predictions, and which is being projected as an autonomous and desirable force. One could also ask: whose future is being predicted? Would the sidewalks that turn pedestrian footfalls into electricity be used in Africa? Will the Indians embrace the 'eco-friendly $345,000, lab-grown, cow-free hamburgers' that nevertheless contain beef? One need not be a technological determinist to appreciate that these predictions present us with a one-dimensional trajectory that actually forecloses the future, which appears as little more than the transformation of society by new technologies. This is the main problem with predictions: they tend to give us a single picture of what is likely to happen on the assumption that there is only one possible future. But the future is pregnant with countless possibilities. The important point to realize is that our future is not predetermined, pre-ordained, or carved out in stone as these predictions seem to suggest; like clay it can be moulded and shaped to our needs and cherished values.

Consider the year 2054. It may turn out as depicted in the science fiction film *Minority Report* (2002), a fascinating exploration of free will and determinism. The film tells the story, or if you like presents a scenario, about 2054 when three bio-engineered young people, 'pre-cogs', are able to foresee murders. They are the main sources of a 'pre-crime' unit, based in Washington D.C., whose officers arrest people for murders they have not yet committed. However, the chief of the unit himself has to go on the run when the pre-cogs foresee him murdering someone he does not know in the near future. The plot turns on the legal and ethical issues involved in imprisoning people for crimes they have not actually committed.

Now, it may be that by 2054 we have developed a technique which tells us what is going to happen before it happens. Many of the technologies depicted in *Minority Report*, such as retinal scanners, electronic gloves, electronic spiders, flying hovercrafts and magnetic levitation may come to fruition. But again they may not. The film assumes that 'technology will continue to be developed and deployed in advanced ways, but not everyone will benefit from it. Also, our world will, of course, be different half a century hence, but some things will remain more or less as they are now, a point illustrated by the fact that business people are still dressing in suits and ties like those they wear today. Similarly, the drugs may change, but drug addiction won't.'[3]

But we can also make other equally viable assumptions. *Minority Report* offers us one possible picture of what might happen in 2054. But there are other possible futures for this particular date. In fact, there are countless alternative futures, possible or desirable, for 2054.

This is why when we systematically explore and research the future we don't actually study 'the future': we study *futures*, with the accent firmly on the plural. The singular term, 'the future', focuses our attention on only one future, has serious political implications and is conceptually rather limited. In contrast, the pluralization of futures, to use the words of the World Futures Studies Federation, 'opens up the territory for envisioning and creating alternative and preferred futures'.[4] Hence, the field of inquiry that critically investigates futures is best described as 'futures studies' (the appellation emphasises both the plurality of futures as well as the plurality of approaches to studying futures), sometimes reduced simply to 'futures'. Those who engage in futures studies (academics and researchers, experts and professionals, activists and consultants) or futures are called futurists.

Beyond positivism

The field of futures studies is the last bastard child of positivism growing up in a postmodern age. It was conceived during the time people believed in a science (predictive and controlling) of the future. We know now that this is not possible (about anything, certainly about the future!).

So we are struggling to find out what futures studies are, given the fact that so many people still want to be able to predict and control the future...Instead of predicting the future, futures studies help people envision and invent the future not as though one were creating an inevitable blueprint, but in order to give a sense of direction and control (not the reality of such) on the assumption that soon after you start heading towards your preferred future, you will experience new things, develop new ideas about a new preferred future, and want to discard the old one.

James Dator, 'Futures studies: today and tomorrow', Futuribili, 1993.

There are, of course, some futurists who specialize in and do little else other than predictions and forecasts. But the majority study alternative futures, examine and imagine different future possibilities, create diverse images and stories about the future, analyse metaphors, myths and underlying assumptions about future worlds, develop methods for exploring futures, critique futures from different cultural, gender and political perspectives, and investigate as wide a range of scenarios and future histories as possible.

The purpose of futures studies is to keep the future open to all alternatives, and to ensure that ideas about the future do not simply become steps towards new forms of oppression. It is as much about the future as it is about our contemporary ideas, feelings, goals,

FUTURES

▲ Jim Dator of The Hawaii Research Center for Futures Studies (image created by his students Cyrus Camp and Aaron Rosa).

vision and desires that might influence the future. It is about foresight and creative management of change. And, above all, it is about present actions, the changes we need to make in our daily lives, everyday practices, social norms and priorities so that we are empowered to usher and shape our preferred future.

The overall message of futures studies, and most futurists, is simple. It is best expressed by Fleetwood Mac's enduring hit:

Don't stop thinking about tomorrow.

It will soon be here.[5]

2

Where is the future?

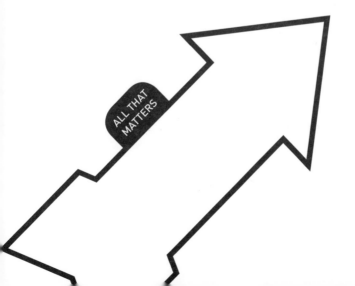

Beyond tomorrow, what are we actually talking about when we talk about the future? We are not talking about the past, a time associated with histories, memories, identity and personal achievements. We are not talking about the present, where we are bogged down with numerous problems and the toil and tribulations of everyday existence. We are thinking and looking forward. But the future extends from now to infinity and talking vaguely about 'the future' does not make much sense. We have to focus on a more meaningful timescale, a period we can study and try to grasp.

For most people, time is continuous, linear and moves in a single direction. Tomorrow invariably follows today, just as today has arrived after yesterday. But not all cultures see time in this particular way. Traditional cultures, for example, see time in terms of cycles: seasons, menstruation and rotation of the moon. Religious traditions such as Hinduism and Buddhism regard time as cyclical, consisting of ages that repeat themselves endlessly: history and future are integrated into a pattern. In some tribal cultures, time and history are related to land: the land decides and creates time, and time is counted according to the activities related to the land. For the Australian aborigines, dreamtime is a sacred era in which ancestral totemic spirits created the world. In some tribal cultures, the notion of time is conspicuous by its absence. For example, the Pirahã Tribe, located in the Amazon rainforest, do not have a notion of the past or the future. Everything exists in the present; it does not exist if it is not here right now. The language of the Brazilian tribe of the Amondawa has no word for time or for time periods such as month or year. As perceptions of time are shaped by culture, we do not have a unitary, uniform, worldwide understanding of time. People relate to time differently and problems can arise between cultures from their different relationships to time.

Auden on Time

Time will say nothing but I told you so,

Time only knows the price we have to pay;

If I could tell you I would let you know.

W.H. Auden

Our perception of time shapes our lives as well as society even though we give little thought to what time is and what it may mean for us. In the Arabian peninsula, for example, life is organized around daily ritual prayer. When someone says they will meet you after *asr* (afternoon) prayer, they mean anytime between *asr* prayer and *maghrib* (evening) prayer – a period of four to five hours. In Central Africa, people make appointments based on the activities of the most common animal in their society: cows. When someone makes a late afternoon appointment, they say 'I will see you when the cows are out'. If a train arrives one minute after scheduled time in Japan, it is late. But in Britain even if it is late by a few minutes it is still 'on time'. In western societies, 'time is money'. But in most Latin American countries time and money are independent quantities. Just because you have a lot of time on your hands, it does not mean it should be devoted exclusively to work. You can give 'time to time' (*dar tiempo al tiempo*), as suggested by a Mexican saying, and have a siesta. In Indian religious traditions and philosophies, such as Hinduism and Buddhism, time is regarded as cyclic, consisting of repeated ages and often depicted as a wheel, for example, at the famous thirteenth-century Konark Sun Temple in Odisha.

▲ A wheel from the Konark Sun Temple, Odisha, signifying the cyclic nature of time; it is used by the government of India as its official symbol and also appears on some currency notes of Indian rupees.

How we view time thus shapes not just our personal lives but also our social relationships, economic and professional activities, and how our societies are structured and function. And it influences our ideas about the future and the kind of future worlds we would like to inhabit.

Given our current, global experience of time as a linear phenomenon, we may dismiss cyclic notions of time as the sole preserve of traditional societies. But cyclic time has played an important part in history, and some historians have described the rise and fall of civilizations in cyclic terms. The Muslim historian Ibn Khaldun (1332–1406), for example, described four stages in the rise and fall of families, culture and civilizations.[1] The first generation creates and innovates. The second generation produces by observing the first. The third generation just imitates. The fourth generation does nothing and simply lives off the wealth, which it sees as its rightful inheritance, of previous generations. The wealth evaporates; creativity disappears. And the cycle has to repeat itself. Similarly, the British historian Arnold Toynbee (1889–1975) described 21 civilizations in the known history of the world, rising and falling in response to challenges.[2] When confronted by an extreme challenge, a creative minority produces solutions that reorient the entire society and lead to the rise of its civilization. But when creative responses to new challenges are not available, discord within society spreads, a despotic minority takes control and the civilization declines. More recently, historian and political scientist Paul Kennedy (1945–) has argued that economic strength and military power have led to the rise and fall of nations since 1500 in cyclic fashion.[3] What happened to the imperial power of Spain, France and Britain would inevitably happen to the Soviet Union (which it did) and the United States.

Eliot on Time

Time present and time past

Are both perhaps present in time future,

And time future contained in time past.

If all time is eternally present

All time is unredeemable.

T.S. Eliot

Historic cycles therefore exert tremendous pressure on the future. We can see cycle-like phenomenon in the global capitalist economy. The economy seems to move in cycles consisting of periods of high growth followed by periods of relatively slow growth. These cycles are called Kondratiev waves after the Russian economist Nikolai Kondratiev (1892–1938), who was the first to notice them. Kondratiev waves are 'characterised by accelerating rates of price increase from deflationary depressions (the 1840s and the 1890s) to inflationary peaks (1815, 1865, 1920), followed by decade-long plunges from the peaks to primary troughs (1825, 1873, 1929), by weak recoveries, and then sags into the next deflationary depressions'.[4]

Kondratiev long waves range from approximately 40 to 60 years, a period in the future that most people would regard as somewhat distant. In contrast, economic forecasts tend to be limited to three months (quarter) or at best to one or two years. Market research is restricted to a range of one to three years. Development forecasts are limited to five years; most developing countries and emerging nations tend to plan in five-year chunks, the maximum period a government stays in power in a democratic society without facing elections. But there is little we can change in a five-year period; perhaps that is why development plans never really work. What, then, would be a more appropriate period to consider?

Let us begin at the beginning: now. The present can be this moment, this hour, today. But the present also incorporates a future that will be, more or less, like the present. It is the future for which economic forecasts are made and development plans are initiated, and during which new models of existing technologies make an appearance, the economy is tinkered with and tuned, policy initiatives are enacted, the current party in power continues on its merry way and fashion changes as it always does. But barring a 'wild card' – a surprising event with significant and radical consequences[5] – nothing much changes. This is the *near future*, which is basically an *extended present*. This future is stable, with discernible trends, and can be known. Most reliable forecasts concentrate on this period. It is the domain of the *predictive future*.

Lawrence on Time

Not I, not I, but the wind that blows through me!

A fine wind is blowing the new direction of time.
D.H. Lawrence

▶ Taking a train

Beyond that is a 10-year horizon where things can change quite significantly. And a decade further on – that is, 20 years from now – almost anything can change. But more importantly anything can be done. Today's actions and decisions may not change the world in the next five years. But they could radically transform the world in the next 20 years, a period pregnant with social, cultural, technological and political transformations.

The 20-year horizon, or the 'mid-term future', presents us with an array of possibilities and potentials. Unlike the extended present which is mostly *a priori* given, it is a place of imagination and will, a space that we can actually alter and shape. Think of the mid-term future as a special railway station, representing the present, from where you can take trains to different destinations in the future. What would be your options? Where would you go? On the basis of data, information and knowledge available at the stations (the present), we can say you have three general possibilities. There are 'possible futures', the amalgam of different possibilities you can imagine. Among these there will be 'probable futures', which have a higher probability of being realized, some of which could become 'plausible futures', that is they are more likely to occur. But there is another more specific option: the actual direction you would like to travel, or 'preferable futures' you embrace. What you prefer depends on a number of things, including the values you hold; the virtues such as justice, equality and compassion which you cherish; the emphasis you place on technological developments and environmental issues; the importance you give to the pressing issues of politics, culture and society. So your preferred futures, your destination, would be a function of your outlook and worldview.

But, of course, you are not alone on the station: there are also many other passengers. Their destinations, or preferred futures, would depend on their own cultural values, cosmologies and priorities. What would happen if there was only one train on the station that could go in a number of different directions? There would be a great deal of negotiation, arguments and attempts at persuasion. Given human nature, there will be some people who would want to impose their will on others,

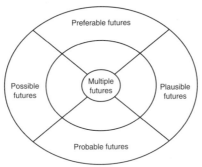

▲ Varieties of futures.

and insist that their preferred future is *the* future of everyone. The future is not immune from colonization.

While the mid-term future provides us with a plethora of alternatives, it is a contested space. Perspectives on alternative futures are as diverse as humanity. Some would emphasize their individual values, beliefs and philosophic priorities: 'personal futures'. Some would give importance to their histories, customs and traditions: 'cultural futures'. Others may stress the importance of their country or region: the futures of 'my nation', European futures, futures of Asia, futures of communities. The more altruistic may place an accent on futures of the poor, refugees and migrants, or global futures. Some would argue from a disciplinary perspective and highlight economic futures, political futures and sociological futures. There will always be those who prefer 'technological futures', or 'feminist futures', or 'spiritual futures'. Proponents of these different perspectives would wish to travel towards their own preferred futures. There has to be a lot of give and take if we all want to travel roughly in the same direction.

All these different varieties of futures are equally valid and all are studied and explored by futures studies and futurists. But a natural question arises: is there a way to reconcile the plethora of mid-term futures? One possibility is to move beyond individual concerns and to think about the consequences of our actions on future generations. Just as we have moral commitments to people alive today – not to kill or harm them, destroy their environment, or undermine their potential – we have exactly the same responsibilities towards future people, who are in no way morally different from us. Indeed, most cultures and traditions agree that we have moral obligations to ensure that future generations not only survive but, just like us, thrive in a viable and healthy planetary environment. This approach focuses our attention on the consequences not just of our current decisions and actions but also of our own 'desirable futures' – after all, a future based on our own (selfish) desires could have serious costs for future generations.

▶ Bon voyage

Thinking about future generations takes us beyond the 20-year horizon of mid-term futures. It takes between 20 and 30 years for a new generation to emerge. Considering that our children and grandchildren could live to a ripe old age, we ought to be thinking in terms of 100 years. Elise Boulding (1920–2010), American sociologist and futurist, has suggested that we should look not just 100 years in front of us but also 100 years before us. This period of 200 years connects us to our grandparents and parents, who have passed on their experiences to us, and to our children and grandchildren, who will inherit what we leave behind. This is temporal space that we actually inhabit, move around in, and in which we touch and are touched by people around us, young and old. The future, in this multigenerational perspective, as Australian futurist Richard Slaughter has argued, becomes a mirror image of the past: our children and grandchildren take the place of our parents and grandparents. This makes the 'far futures' of 100 years, with its personal and family commitments, rather immediate.[6] You cannot afford to overlook it if you take your responsibilities to yourself and your children's children seriously. You will have a direct impact on their lives the way you live now.

Our potential directions of travel multiply rapidly with a 100-year horizon. Within this period, civilizations can decay and disappear, climate can change drastically, flora and fauna can become extinct, totally new social values can emerge, even our notion of what it means to be human can change radically. Now, you are not at a station, limited to rail tracks, but standing on a port: the future is an ocean. You can sail in *any* direction. But you still need a sense of direction, an idea, a vision, of where you want to go, and some navigational equipment to get you to your destination.

We can go further and think about 200 or 300, or even 1,000 years from now. This is the *Star Trek* future as 'Space: The Final Frontier'. Such 'deep futures', as they are known, are mostly an arena of speculation, well explored by science fiction. We can imagine human possibilities in the year 3000, wonder where contemporary trends and developments will take us, ponder how innovations and inventions such as genetic engineering, merging of biology and information and space travel would or could shape and transform humanity. Most of the questions we raise about deep futures tend to be about the threats to human survival. Can humanity survive global climate change, pandemics, water scarcity, soil erosion or species extinction? What are the risks of runaway nanotechnology, the emergence of super-intelligences or a collision with an asteroid? What is the probability that humans could become extinct within the next 1,000 years? Nobody knows: deep futures are truly unknowable. But that does not mean we can't speculate, generate and critically examine ideas about distant futures, or create images and models of what the long-distance future could be.

Futures studies explore all these time horizons and concerns itself with all the issues of humanity.

A short history of
futures studies

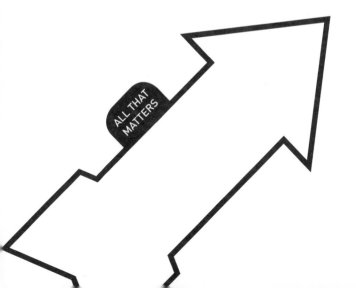

Humanity has always been fascinated by the future. Astrology probably made an appearance at the same time as *homo sapiens* learned to walk, looked at the sky and wondered what it all meant. Ancient Greek mythology is full of oracles who, inspired by gods, could predict the future. The classic Chinese text, *I Ching*, which predates recorded history, contains a mystical system of divination and prediction. When ancient cultures built monuments, they built for the future. Think of the pyramids in Giza, or the monuments of the Maya and Aztec civilizations. But it wasn't all mythology and mysticism.

The Greek philosopher Heraclitus (535–475 BC) believed that 'everything flows' and 'nothing remains still'; change and transformations are the only constant. The historian Thucydides (460–395 BC) was also a keen student of change. He observed the changes around him and noticed that the character of change was also changing and wrote about cultural changes which might emerge in another generation. Many Greek philosophers thought in utopian terms. In the *Republic*, for example, Plato (427–347 BC) argued for a future world based on justice as the principle of power and authority. St Augustine (354–430) built a future *City of God* based on love in contrast to a city of earth based on pride. The Muslim philosopher and physician Ibn Sina (980–1037) imagined a future world based on the liberated intellect where rationality was supreme. In his novel *The Life of Hayy*, Ibn Taufyl (1105–85) placed his protagonist, who spontaneously emerges from the slime, on a desert island in an attempt to show how such a world can be created. The philosopher Ibn Rushd (1126–1198) argued that, apart from God, only human intellect was eternal and the future should be guided by it.

Utopian views of the future come of age with Thomas More's (1478–1535) *Utopia*. More imagines a future society based on common good, where the community is much more important than the individual. Based on the romanticized notion of the people of the 'New World', the indigenous tribes of America, *Utopia* nevertheless demonstrated a commitment to change to what More imagined was a better future. In sharp contrast, Francis Bacon (1561–1626) constructed an ideal state, based on individualism and the power of men, in his *New Atlantis*. Utopian exploration of the future continued with the French novelist Louis-Sébastien Mercier (1740–1814). Inspired by the German philosopher and mathematician Gottfried Wilhelm von Leibniz (1646–1716), who declared 'the present is pregnant with the future', Mercier imagined a futuristic Paris in his *The Year 2040*. Subtitled 'A Dream If Ever There Was One', the novel had its protagonist dreaming about a Paris of the future and offered some highly original insights. It became very popular and went through scores of editions.

More recent science fiction, both utopian and dystopian, from writers ranging from Mary Shelley, Jules Verne and H.G. Wells to George Orwell, Aldous Huxley, Arthur C. Clarke, Stanislaw Lem, Isaac Asimov, Philip K. Dick and Ursula LeGuin, has turned our gaze towards the future.

However, a more disciplined approach to the study of the future, based on systematic research using quantitative and qualitative methods, did not emerge until the late

1950s. And it emerged simultaneously in the United States and in France.

▶ Contested claims

In the US, the study of the future began at the RAND Corporation, an institution that was an integral part of what President Eisenhower described in 1961 as the 'military-industrial complex'. RAND was established as an independent think tank in 1948 to undertake research and development work for the US armed forces, and has been instrumental since then in defining American military strategy. During the Cold War, the years following the Second World War, most of the work at RAND concentrated on predicting the patterns of incoming enemy aircrafts and the possible consequences of a nuclear exchange. The notion of deterrence through Mutually Assured Destruction (MAD) was developed at RAND. The institution's chief strategist, Herman Kahn, also came up with the idea of a winnable nuclear exchange; he is said to be one of the models for the character of Dr Strangelove in Stanley Kubrick's 1964 film of the same name.

In 1964, Olaf Helmer and Theodore Gordon, two prominent members of the RAND staff, declared that they had discovered a general theory of prediction that could 'deal with socio-economic and political problems as confidently as we do with problems in physics and chemistry'.[1] The arrival of computers meant that vast amounts of information about trends and developments could now be processed methodically. Researchers now had the same capability, Helmer and Gordon claimed, that 'in the physical sciences, created the breakthrough which led to the development of the atomic bomb'. The future was now liberated from the grip of utopias and superstitions and had become a science.

What Helmer and Gordon had produced was a systematic and disciplined method for forecasting. But it could hardly be compared with theories and methods of physics and chemistry. Their prediction technique came to be known as the Delphi method of forecasting. It involves asking a group of anonymous experts a selected list of key questions about the future: what is the probability of a nuclear war, landing a mission on Mars, or discovering an elixir for eternal youth? The questions are asked in a number of phases, each phase refining the question from the previous phase, and the experts are given an opportunity to examine and modify their previous answers. Finally, an attempt is made to attain a consensus, usually measured in terms of a probability and feasibility of a particular event occurring in the future. It is all rather subjective – as opinions, including opinions of experts, usually are – but a fair degree of consensus among the experts contributing to the survey gives it an air of objectivity.

Despite its limitations, Delphi initiated a boom in forecasting. The 'new science of the future' was dubbed 'futurology', and was eagerly embraced by US government organizations, corporations and certain universities, and promoted by institutions such as RAND, the Congress for Cultural Freedom and the Ford Foundation. Within five years, there was a global boom in 'futurology': commissions, institutes and government departments for long-range and future planning were established in Europe, Japan, the (then) Soviet Union, the (Communist) countries of Eastern Europe, and many developing countries.

Futurology also received a boost from the work of Herman Khan, who left RAND Corporation in 1961 to establish the Hudson Institute, named after Croton-on-Hudson, New York, where it was originally located. Kahn was a tactical thinker interested in managing strategic transitions to the future through interdisciplinary studies in defence, international relations, economics and technology. His chosen methodology was not Delphi but trend extrapolations, which he used effectively to predict *The Year 2000*[2] and *The Emerging Japanese Superstate.*[3] Most of his forecasts focused on high technology and extrapolated from the past to the future and contained strong elements of optimism. There was an implicit belief that technology will solve most problems, there will be continuous economic growth and things will get better and better for America. In 1966 a group of academics, consultants, businessmen and writers, interested in how social and technological developments were shaping the future, came together to establish the World Future Society in Washington D.C.

The term 'futurology' was already in circulation by the time the RAND study on Delphi was published. It was coined in 1943 by Ossip Flechtheim, who was born in Ukraine, taught in Germany, and ended up in exile in New York. But for Flechtheim the study of the future had little to do with predictions: it was a territory contested by different utopian visions, and 'futurology' was all about systematic reflection on the present.[4]

Europe had other ideas too. There was an established custom of long-range planning in France, Britain, Austria, Norway and Holland, and an age-old tradition of utopian thinking, particularly in France where it was associated with thinkers such as Henri de Saint-Simon (1716–1825), Auguste Comte (1798–1857) and Condorcet (1743–1794). This rich heritage was well utilized by Gaston Berger (1896–1960), an industrialist and philosopher born in Senegal, to develop a more nuanced approach to the future. Berger coined the term 'prospective' to emphasize that the future is both deterministic and free, passively suffered but also actively willed. In 1957, Berger established the Centre International de Prospective in Paris, and, a year later, launched *Prospective*, a journal devoted to the study of the future.

In Holland, the Dutch thinker Frederik Polak had been working on the perceptions of the future in western civilization for some years. His classic work *The Image of the Future* was published in 1955, and argues that both the Renaissance and Marxism are products of particular images of the future.[5] A year earlier, Robert Jungk, Austrian writer and social critic, had published *Tomorrow is Already Here*, which examined the potential horrors of nuclear weapons.[6]

During the 1960s, Europe boosted a thriving community of scholars, scientists and philosophers devoted to studying the future, all with an impressive list of publications. At about the same time that RAND published its study on Delphi, a seminal work by the French philosopher Bertrand de Jouvenel (1903–1987) appeared in Paris offering a systematic and philosophical rationale for the exploration of the future. It brought the differences between the American and European approaches to the future into a sharp focus. While the Americans described 'futurology' as a science, de Jouvenel called his book *The Art of Conjecture*.[7] The American approach accentuated 'the future' and presented it as a close, deterministic space; de Jouvenel emphasized choice and talked about possible futures which could be built by our imagination leading to a humane world of preferences. He rejected the label 'futurology' and used the term 'futuribles', placing the accent firmly on possible plural futures that could emerge from the present. De Jouvenel went on to establish a network of scholars working in the futures field and organized a number of conferences on the methodologies of futures thinking. He founded the Paris-based Association Internationale de Futuribles, from where he published the journal *Futuribles*.

By the late 1960s, doubts about the security and corporate approach to the future had begun to emerge even in the US. Among the doubters were ecologist and futurist John McHale and Hasan Ozbekhan, a Turkish-American philosopher and planner, who worked on global problems. McHale saw the future as open-ended. While he acknowledged that prediction is an important element of the exploration of the future, he tended to emphasize conjecture, imaginative extrapolation and normative projection. The study of the future, he suggested, should focus on the long term, delineate power relationships, take into account cultural values and reach out for alternatives; it should promote choice and freedom.

Ozbekhan argued that technology was not value neutral; a future based solely on technological projections promoted the norms and values of the society where technology first emerged. Moreover, technology had serious downsides too and a notion of the future based solely on technology seriously threatened the planet itself. In 1968, Ozbekhan joined hands with the Italian industrialist Aurelio Peccei to set up the Club of Rome, a global network of the great and the good 'sharing a common concern for the future of humanity'. Ozbekhan became the first Director of the Club and influenced its decision to address issues of environmental degradation, resource depletion, overpopulation and energy. The Club's 1972 first report, *The Limits to Growth*,[8] garnered considerable public attention and concern for these issues. It provided an interesting contrast to the popular literature on the future such as Alvin Toffler's *Future Shock*,[9] which argued that humanity is moving from industrial society to a 'super-industrial society'.

But in Europe, visions of 'super-industrial society' were greeted with scepticism. The disenchantment with the American approach to the future had become widespread by the late 1960s. A special issue on futurology of UNESCO's *International Social Science Journal*, published in 1969 with contributions from Jungk, Igor Bestuzhev-Lada, a Russian historian and expert in forecasting, and many Eastern European scholars implicitly criticized the Delphi method. 'Committees of wise men', it stated, 'try to predict coming discoveries, on the basis of their knowledge of science and a list of research projects in progress' but their function is not different from 'those responsible for drawing up research programmes' in the first place.[10] In other words Delphi was simply reflecting the interests of the research community dressed up as 'predictions'. The European futurists were not only questioning the scientific status of 'futurology' but they also connected it to international political and economic developments.

Both Jungk and Bestuzhev-Lada were involved in an 'international committee' of scholars, social scientists and futures thinkers from Western and Eastern Europe, the Soviet Union and Japan who wished to create an 'international futures research movement'. Set up at the initiative of Jungk, it was called Mankind 2000, and included de Jouvenel, McHale, Johan Galtung, a Norwegian sociologist and expert on conflict studies, and Mahdi Elmandjra, a Moroccan economist and futurist who was Deputy Director of UNESCO, among its members. Between 1969 and 1972, Mankind 2000 organized a number of 'future research inaugural conferences' in Oslo, Rome, Bucharest and Kyoto, where the epistemological and political issues of the study of the future were hotly debated and courses were provided for students and young scholars. The first Oslo meeting spelled out the concerns of the participants:

▲ Cover of UNESCO's *International Scoial Science Journal* special issue on futurology.

In calling a conference dedicated to peace and development in the next decades, the organizers pointed to a new and urgent direction of future research. Could the new intellectual tools of information technology, systems analysis, operational research, forecasting, anticipating, scenario writing and 'futures creation' be used on civilian problems? These new powerful tools should not be restricted to technocratic elite, for the future belongs to all of us and for that reason it is absolutely essential that future research is internationalized and democratized as quickly as possible.[11]

During its 1972 Conference in Bucharest, Mankind 2000 decided to establish a 'permanent worldwide organisation' devoted to promoting 'futures-oriented thinking in all branches of knowledge and action'. This move was motivated not just by the American approach to the future, but also by the activities of the Washington D.C.-based World Future Society (WFS), which many saw as a business, promoting a monolithic technological vision of the future. A more pluralistic approach to the future, taking into account the hopes and aspirations of the world's diverse non-western cultures, it was argued, could not emerge from an institution which consisted mostly of Americans and was located in 'the Belly of the Beast and supported by many of the Beast's feeders and coddlers'. Among those who attended the Bucharest meeting were the Italian futurist Eleonora Masini and the American political scientist and futurist Jim Dator – both were to play an important part in developing a more pluralistic understanding of the future. The participants, Dator later recalled, asked: 'do we really want to foist our hates and fears on the rest of the world? Aren't there many alternative futures out there, in the hearts and minds of silenced cultures worldwide, that we should seek out and nourish?' What was needed, they suggested, was a futures organization 'which would embrace honestly and proudly the vast diversity of images, hopes, and fears of the future. It would strive to be the incubator for local and global visions for a peaceful, equitable, and cooperative world.'[12]

▶ The Federation

The organization was duly established, with the support of UNESCO, at the 1973 conference in Paris. It was called 'World Futures Studies Federation'. Bertrand de Jouvenel became the Founding President, followed soon afterwards by John Galtung as the first President. It was housed in de Jouvenel's institution, Maison Internationale Futuribles, in Paris. The name of the institution was significant. The new organization, in contrast to the WFS, was a 'Federation' not just of national academic bodies and institutions but also of individual futurists: the Fellows. The Federation not only shunned the term 'futurology' but also placed an accent on futures to emphasize plurality and alternatives. 'Futures studies', adopted after much debate and discussion, was meant to incorporate the terms forecasting and perspective, as well as the term 'prognostic', widely used in Eastern European countries to indicate that moment of thinking about the future which precedes the action of planning. The Federation, its constitution declared, was devoted to 'the stimulation, exchange, and examination of ideas, visions, and plans for alternative, long-term futures'. When Galtung retired as the President of the Federation, he was succeeded by Elmandjra, and then in 1981 by Masini who has come to be regarded as the 'doyen' of futures studies. In 1990, Dator took over as President of the Federation. Together, Masini and Dator have trained a whole generation of futurists.

The intellectual struggle for pluralising the future undertaken by those involved in the Federation was not without tensions and acute differences of opinion. Quite a few scholars from Japan and the Communist bloc had a very positivist and singular approach to the future. Futurists from 'Japan Society of Futurology' consistently argued for 'a vision of a high-tech society, to which the existing societal institutions should adapt'.[13] The Russians fought for their Marxist-Leninist vision of the future, and, not infrequently, their delegates to futures conferences of the 1970s tended to be Party officials. Dator describes an event at the seminal 1972 Bucharest conference:

A group of us met in a small room nearby every day to hammer out a draft constitution for the Federation. The participants were an impressively diverse group of futurists from Eastern and Western Europe, the US, and Asia. But the people we knew as futurists in the USSR were somehow not in attendance. Instead, sitting in silence in the corner, smoking endlessly and in general acting as though he were 'The Communist From Hollywood's Central Casting', was someone from the Soviet Union. He spoke not a word during our meetings. But on the last day of the Conference, when the draft WFSF constitution was being presented to the participants in a plenary session, the Communist From Central Casting jumped to his feet, raced down the parquet-squeaking floor, mounted the stage and (without actually taking his shoes off) did his best imitation of Khrushchev Haranguing the Capitalists: 'Why do you call this organization the "World Futures Studies Federation?" It is Future, not FutureS. There is only one future: Ours. There are no alternative futures! You must erase the "S" from World Futures Studies Federation and make it properly the World Future Studies Federation, or no socialist country will become a member '.[14]

There were other numerous competing perspectives, from India, the Arab and Muslim world, Latin America and Africa, all implicitly incorporating critiques of the dominant positions. Indian futurists stressed the value-laden nature of futures thinking. Rajni Kothari, a leading futurist who established the Delhi-based Centre for Developing Societies, argued for a workable approach to the future under imperfect conditions to seek a future which was better than the present.

The futurist faces a dilemma, Kothari wrote in his seminal 1974 book *Footsteps into the Future*:[15] to be guided by those fundamental credo that leave the past behind and remould the present towards a different world; or be sceptical about a total break with the past, which is both an impossible and a dangerous proposition. A strategy was needed that appreciated the value of Indian traditions and incorporated the rich history of the Sub-Continent in the futures framework.

In a 1983 study called *Images of Arab Future*[16] social scientists and futurists from the Middle East complained of being misrepresented by global models of the future, such as those developed by the Club of Rome for *The Limits to Growth* and subsequent studies such as *Mankind and Turning Point*.[17] Arab futures, it claimed, cannot be divorced from the history of the region and can only be envisaged in 'the very long term'. The Arabs must develop their own approach to the future, which must be liberated from oil and turmoil. There were also arguments for the study of the future from a civilizational perspective. *The Future of Muslim Civilization*,[18] which appeared in 1979, argued for an egalitarian, non-consumer oriented perspective on the future. It took a systems approach to the past and present of Muslim people within a cultural context and suggested that we were heading towards a multi-civilizational world.

In contrast, the Latin American futurists dismissed the long-term forecast of the state of humanity as ideologically biased, and argued for a more participatory, basic needs approach. Explorations of the future, they suggested in a famous 1976 study *Catastrophe or New Society? A Latin American World Model*,[19] should focus on basic needs such as food, housing, education and employment. Basic needs were also the focus of African futures. A 1986 study entitled *Reclaiming the Future*, based on numerous workshops and conferences held throughout Africa, defined futures studies 'first and foremost as a state of mind' which 'calls for an integrated *demarche* and a long-term vision of alternative choices and an awareness of their respective implications'.[20] Africa should not be an appendage to western futures, it argued, but should explore its own futures based on its own values focusing on such areas as food self-sufficiency, rural and human resource development, regional security and human rights.

By the 1980s, the debate on what it means to study and explore the future had become global and methods of studying the future had multiplied manifold. Different approaches to futures in different parts of the world had created different traditions of futures studies. The terminology, concepts and the methods of understanding, forecasting or imagining futures that have emerged are deeply rooted in this historical process.

▲ Futurists who made history: Bertrand de Jouvenel (left), Herman Kahn (middle) and Eleonora Masini (right).

Terminology, principles, concepts

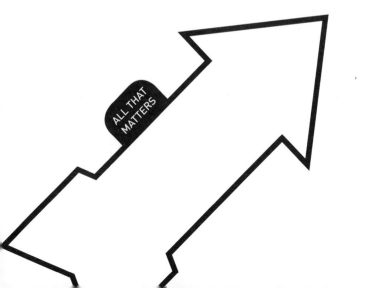

The historic struggle has produced an overabundance of terms for the exploration and study of the future. While 'futurology' is frequently used in the popular press, it is limited to a narrow circle of American academics and scholars. Other terms such as 'futuristics', 'futurism' and 'futuring' have also been used. Futuristics was in vogue during the 1970s but has now disappeared. Futurism has also been used sometimes, mostly by American writers. But it is a misnomer: it is associated, and was used by, the far-right radical art movement that flourished in Italy during the early twentieth century. The rather ugly term 'futuring' is still used, largely by the American World Future Society, to describe the process of actively envisioning the future. But the most widely used term in the US is futures study. In continental Europe, particularly in France and Spain, the study of the future still goes under the rubric of 'prospective'. The most commonly used term, however, is futures studies.

Other designations have emerged over the last decade. As futures exploration became popular in corporations and in business and marketing circles, a number of terms emerged with a specific focus on management: 'scenario planning', 'strategic management', 'strategic foresight'. All these terms basically describe a practical approach to the future. Scenario planning, for example, is simply a mode of inquiry and analysis that uses scenarios to enhance the understanding of the future and support planning. A relatively new term that coalesces these different organization-based activities is 'foresight'.

Foresight was first coined by the science fiction writer H.G. Wells (1866–1946), who wanted the world to prepare for things to come. Wells lamented the fact that 'we did nothing to our roads until they were chocked; we did nothing to adjust our railroads to fit in with this new element in life until they were overtaken and bankrupt; we have still to bring our police up to date with the motor bandit. That is what I mean by want of Foresight.' In a famous BBC broadcast, Wells called for Professors of Foresight 'who make a whole-time job of estimating the future consequences of new inventions and new devices'.[1] Foresight, which came into vogue during the first decade of the twenty-first century and is now widely used in management circles and business schools, focuses on what might happen within an organization so better decisions can be made to manage risks and contingency. It is sometimes used as a substitute for futures studies, but is more accurately regarded as a subset of futures studies focused on organizational futures.

To compound the confusion, the term 'forecast' is sometimes used as a substitute for 'the future'. The confusion arose when forecasting was seen as the only methodology for studying the future. But nowadays it is considered as merely one tool among many. Worse: 'forecast' and 'prediction' are often used as synonyms in futures literature. But, I think, it is important to differentiate between the two. A prediction is a statement about a future state of affairs, and is often calendar bound. We make informal predictions almost every day. But to have any real use and meaning, a prediction has to be confined to a system that can be measured and understood; for example, the fuel needed for a plane to fly to a particular destination, the possibility of an earthquake in a region, or the possible outcome of a general election.

Various terms used to describe the study of the future

'conditional future contingents' (Luis de Molina, 1589)

'social mathematics' (Concordet, 1804)

'Kondratiev long waves' (Nikolai Kondratiev, 1930s)

'foresight' (H.G. Wells, 1932)

'scenarios approach' (RAND, 1940s)

'futurology' (Ossip K. Flechtheim, 1946)

'futurible' (Bernard de Jouvenel, 1950s)

'prospective analysis' (Gaston Berger, 1957)

'futures studies' (World Futures Studies Federation, early 1960s)

'futures research' (World Future Society, 1960)

'strategic management' (various schools, since 1960s)

'futures study' (World Future Society, 1970s)

'strategic foresight' (Richard Slaughter, 1995)

'futuring' (Ed Cornish, Jerry Glenn, 2004)

Forecasts, on the other hand, are based on certain hypotheses that are carefully constructed from analysis of past experiences or events. If the hypothesis is valid, current trends continue, and certain initial conditions hold – not likely, given the rapidity with which things change – we can put a high level of confidence in the forecast. A prediction does not have to say anything about the state of the future; it just has to state what could or would happen. A forecast has to consider possible changes in the future itself and include a 'what if' process of reasoning: if this happens, then that could happen; if that happens, then something else could happen. A forecast is thus a much more complex statement of probability.

▶ Assumptions and principles

Given the plethora of perspectives on futures studies, it should not surprise us that different scholars ascribe different assumptions and principles to the field. In his seminal work, *Foundations of Futures Studies*, Wendell Bell collates all the suppositions of futures studies into a list of nine 'key assumptions':

1 Time is continuous, unidirectional and irreversible;

2 Not everything that will exist has existed or does exist;

3 Futures thinking is essential for human actions;

4 The most useful knowledge is the 'knowledge of the future';

5 There are no facts about the future;

6 Future is not totally predetermined;

7 To a greater or lesser degree future outcomes can be influenced by individual and collective action;

8 The interdependence in the world invited a holistic perspective and a transdisciplinary approach to the exploration and study of the future as well as for the organization of knowledge for decision-making and social action; and

9 Some futures are better than others.[2]

We can have knowledge of forecasts and visions, scenarios and expert opinions, but this is, of course, not the same thing as knowing the future. So what does Bell mean by his suggestion that 'the most useful knowledge is the knowledge of the future'? A modicum of understanding of what the future may hold, Bell explains, is necessary to make goal-oriented decisions:

We steer ourselves through time, as well as physical and social space, according to our goals, our expectations of future happenings, and our anticipations of the possible and probable future time trajectories of other people. The more we know about the possibilities and probabilities of the coming events of the future, the better we are able to plan the actions that create our lives.[3]

Most academics and researchers working in the futures field would base their work on some or all of these assumptions, even if they do not agree that the 'knowledge of future' beats all other varieties of knowledge. But the principles underlying their analysis are more difficult to discern. Eleonora Masini, for example, argues that futures studies are based on three principles: the constant dilemma between knowledge on the one hand, and desire and fear of the future on the other; the realization that the only space on which humans can have an impact is the future; and the appreciation that there is not one future, but many possible futures.[4] In contrast, Dator playfully distils the basic principles into 'Two Laws' of futures studies: 'the future cannot be "predicted" but alternative futures can be "forecasted" and preferred futures "envisioned" and "invented" – continuously'; and 'any *useful idea about the futures should appear to be ridiculous*'.[5] Taking a cue from Dator, I have produced, just as playfully, my own four laws of futures studies. Of course, these are not 'laws' as we understand them: statements that describe, predict and even explain the behaviour of natural phenomenon. Rather, they are general statements that attempt to provide a guiding framework for futures thought and action.

Sardar's four laws of futures studies

Sardar's first law of futures studies: futures studies are wicked.

All futures problems are complex, interconnected, contradictory, located in an uncertain environment and embedded in landscapes that are rapidly changing. Efforts to solve one or a collective of problems often create a plethora of new problems. Such problems are described as 'wicked problems'. But futures studies are wicked not simply because by their very nature they tackle wicked problems; they are also wicked in the sense that they are playfully open-ended, offer not one but a number of possibilities, and their boundaries, such as they are, are totally porous. They are quite happy to borrow ideas and tools, whatever is needed, from any and all disciplines and discourses. Futures studies are wicked in yet another way: while multi- and trans-disciplinary, they are also unashamedly un-disciplinary, that is, futures studies consciously reject the status and state of a discipline while being a fully fledged systematic mode of critical inquiry.

Sardar's second law of futures studies: futures studies are MAD.

The capitals in MAD are important: it is an acronym for Mutually Assured Diversity. Diversity, in all its mindboggling forms, is the essence of what makes us fully human. Mutually assured diversity is the proposition that full preservation of our humanity requires that this diversity is assured, that it not only survives but thrives in any desired future, and that future generations mutually recognize and appreciate each other's diversity. MAD has certain specific requirements for futures studies. First, it requires the recognition that there are different ways to be human, and, as such, different future paths to the full realization of our collective humanity. Second, it requires the appreciation of the fact that the human condition is a cultural condition and that culture is an essential relational attribute, an enabling feature of knowing, being and doing. Given the diversity of cultures on this planet, there are different knowledge systems, different histories, different forms of living, different criteria of accomplishment and different ways of adjusting to change. MAD provides futures studies with the imperative to ensure that the future is assured and remains continuously open to all potentials and possibilities of mutual diversities.

Sardar's third law of futures studies: futures studies are sceptical.

The third law is a natural corollary of the first and second. Futures studies need to be sceptical of simple, one-dimensional solutions to wicked problems as well as of dominant ideas, projections, predictions, forecasts and notions of truth to ensure that the future is not foreclosed and colonized by a single culture. Thus the scepticism of futures studies is not criticism for the sake of criticism but directed towards certain ends: opening up pluralistic potentials. Scepticism in futures studies is an instrument of positive change: it expresses the questions: What else is possible? What other perspectives are there? What impact will this or that future have on others? And ultimately: cui bono? Who benefits from future outcomes of certain trends, developments, projections, forecasts, scenarios or visions? Futures studies are equally sceptical of declarations that suggest that concepts and methods of the discourse will logically lead to true claims about how the future will turn out.

Sardar's fourth law of futures studies: futures studies are futureless.

Futures studies are futureless not in the dictionary sense of 'having no prospect or home of a future'. It does not mean that futures studies will not continue to exist in the far distant future. But futures studies are 'futureless' in a technical, specific sense: since we can have no true knowledge of the future, the impact of all futures explorations can only be meaningfully assessed in the present. We can look back on predictions and forecasts and see how right or how far off the mark they were. But we cannot assess how right or wrong they actually are from the future itself. Thus the real relevance of futures studies lies in the present. All futures activities have a direct impact on the present: they can change peoples' perceptions, make them aware of dangers and opportunities ahead, motivate them to do specific things, force them to invent or innovate, encourage them to change and adjust, galvanize them into collective social action, paralyse them with fear, empower them, marginalize them, or tell them they and their cultures and belief systems are important or unimportant. So ultimately what really matters is the impact futures studies have now; and the value and quality can only be judged in the present.[6]

Many futures concepts place an overall emphasis on decision-making and planning for the future. The four futures concepts developed by Richard Slaughter, for example, focus on an active view of decision-making: 'decisions have long-term consequences', 'future alternatives imply present choices', 'forward thinking is preferable to crisis management' and 'further transformations are certain to occur'. Some of our decisions, says Slaughter, 'powerfully condition the present and the future'. The survival or extinction of entire species, or the viability of our environment, for example, is dependent on our decisions and the lifestyles we choose. As we can envisage many different future possibilities, we have considerable freedom of choice. When we become aware of different alternative futures,

---

we gain access to new choices in the present. If we become aware of something we want to avoid, we can take appropriate action. Similarly, if we can imagine something we want to create, we can set in motion the means to create it. This is as true of a relationship as it is of a new car or airport. Future alternatives imply present choices because it takes time to exert our will and mobilise the resources involved to achieve a given outcome or avoid undesirable consequences.

Thus, rather than move from crisis to crisis, it is far better to think ahead, and plan for the future, while keeping in mind that the future will change and transform continuously and 'the prospective changes over the next hundred years are probably as great as those which have occurred over the last thousand'.[7]

▶ Epistemologies and traditions

Given that the terminology, assumptions, principles and concepts of futures studies have emerged within, and are intrinsically linked to, a historical process, they are not value-free. Along with methods of understanding, forecasting or imagining the future, the terminology and principles of futures studies are epistemological constructions. They are based on various theories of knowledge which are always open to questions and analysis. Much of futures studies is thus about deconstructing and interpreting how individuals and communities, cultures and discourses approach, imagine and try to create the future they desire, the framework of knowledge they employ, the images and metaphors that guide them, and the underlying assumptions of the methods they use. The overall goal is to problematize all approaches and views to the future by asking critical questions: who gains, what are the potential costs and benefits, what ontological and epistemological conventions are being used, is the future on offer inclusive, includes all potential actors, or an exclusive future, limited to certain groups?

Not all futurists bother with such questions. But one who does is the Pakistani/Australian futurist Sohail Inayatullah, a pioneer of the movement for deconstructing the underlying assumptions, epistemologies and cultural biases of the images and metaphors of the future. For Inayatullah, the field of futures studies is an interpretive enterprise, and the ideal theory of the future must be able to problematize time and to negotiate many meanings of time, even as it might be committed to a particular view and construction of time. The fundamental question for the individual engaged in exploring future alternatives is not 'who am I' but 'when am I'.[8] Only by placing oneself within one's own conception of time can one articulate alternative frameworks for understanding the future.

Moreover, every image of the future, Inayatullah suggests, should be integrated with six conceptual questions. Have you purchased a 'used future'? In other words, is your image of the future your desired future or is it unconsciously borrowed from someone else? And, as a result, have you become a victim of the 'disowned future', the future that you desired for yourself but discarded because of influence, because it was swept away by trends or simply because of lack of confidence? By looking at alternative futures you may discover something fresh and have a new vision of the future. But this new vision requires alignment: your day-to-day problem solving and strategy needs to be aligned with the broader vision that you now desire. You also need to have a certain amount of self-belief; if, for example, you think that the future is all doom and gloom and there is nothing you can do about it, you are not going to go very far. You need to think about the model of social change you have embraced. Is it optimistic or pessimistic, does it see time as linear or cyclical, or the future as already determined by technology or prophecy? Finally, you need to think of the use of the future: how are you going to use your vision, your understanding of possible alternatives, to create a more effective strategy for the future you desire?[9] Inyatullah's concepts force us to reflect critically on our own assumptions as well as to question all those things about the future that we take for granted.

The terminology, principles and concepts that I have outlined are not used, or indeed accepted, universally. Different traditions of future studies often use different terms and employ diverse principles and notions. To evaluate or understand a particular exploration of the future, say a forecast or a vision, it is necessary to appreciate the tradition in which it is embedded. The overall 'futures field', that is, the broad-based, complex and international area of study that takes futures concerns as its main focus, is based on five distinct traditions, ably summarized by the World Futures Studies Federation:

- The 'empirical tradition', which focuses on trend analysis, prediction and forecasts, began with work at RAND Corporation and the Hudson Institute, was popularized by the World Future Society, and is the dominant tradition in the US.

- The 'critical tradition', which emerged in Europe through the works of Bertrand de Jouvenel, Frederik Polak, Robert Jungk and others and grew out of a critique of what was perceived as an overly empirical approach to futures in the USA. It recognizes that knowledge and narratives of the future, as well as their interpretations, have a politics and can have hegemonic tendencies.

▶ The 'cultural tradition', which arose from the works of non-western futurists such as Rajni Kothari, the Indian psychologist and futurist Ashis Nandy, the Latin American futurist Antonio Alonso Concheiro and many African futurists, seeks to pluralize all approaches to futures, keep the future open to all dissenting possibilities and invoke a deeper consideration of civilizational and planetary futures.

▶ The 'empowerment-oriented' action research approach began in Europe in the 1990s and has been taken up by some Australian researchers.

▶ The 'integral/transdisciplinary' futures approach developed recently to make explorations of the future more inclusive, diverse and empowering.[10]

Of course, these traditions are not mutually exclusive. One could, for example, undertake an empirical study that incorporates both cultural and critical perspective. But the five traditions do reflect well-established paths of both research and teaching in futures studies. A postgraduate course in futures studies at an American university will tend to emphasize empirical work, while another at an Australian university will focus on integral and action-oriented futures.

A great deal of what goes under the rubric of 'futures research', in contrast to futures studies, in corporations, government planning departments, business schools and international organizations, is focused on empirical work that aims to predict and control the future through planning. The people who work in this area tend to be specialists in forecasting and planning who use sophisticated analytical and quantitative methods. 'Futures consultants' help businesses, organizations, communities and governments to envision viable futures and facilitate in developing goals, plans and strategies towards a desired future. Consultants tend to have expertise in a number of areas and freely borrow concepts and methodologies from different traditions depending on the context of their work. There are also 'futures movements' concerned with raising issues about the future, empowering communities, and shaping more socially just, inclusive and pluralistic futures. Individuals involved in such movements may not even consider themselves to be futurists but they use methodologies and analytical techniques developed within the critical, cultural and empowerment-oriented traditions of futures studies.

5

Looking forward

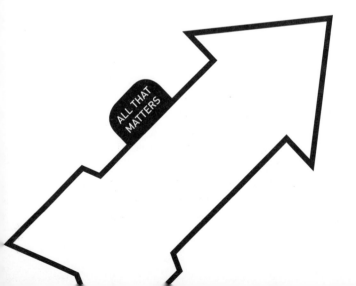

Given its distinct and diverse traditions, it should not surprise us to know that futures studies are rich in methodologies. Some methods have emerged from within the field itself, such as Delphi and other forecasting techniques, and have played an important part in the evolution and in defining the character of futures studies. But futures studies also borrow methods from other disciplines in sciences, social sciences and humanities. As an interdisciplinary and transdisciplinary field, it has freely borrowed methodological techniques from existing disciplines if they are relevant to the study of the future.

The most common and widely used methods look forward towards the future. These methods start from the present, using the information and data available, to predict or forecast a future over which we have little or no influence. The methods for 'foreseeing' the future can be objective (grounded in empirical work) or normative (mission oriented), and use variables (that is things that are likely to change) and indicators (important quantitative or qualitative factors) to describe the existing reality. We cannot change the future that is forecast, but we can prepare for it.

The most commonly used method for forecasting is 'trend extrapolation'. Trends relating to a specific area, for example the economy, population or energy use, are examined to see how they will develop in the future. Quantitative data is collected for a period of time and scrutinized to see if any recognisable patterns are present. Variables are inspected to determine if there are correlations between two or more variables. Leading indicators are identified and studied. Trend extrapolation can be quite simple, with virtually no theoretical understanding, offering no explanation of changes in the variables as well as exceptionally sophisticated involving detailed mathematical and statistical analysis. But all involve four basic steps: (1) data collection, (2) plotting the data on a graph, (3) identifying the pattern and (4) projecting the trend.

The end result can have a number of possibilities. The trends can be constant, with periodic additions and subtractions, but remaining within a boundary, in which nothing much will change in the future. They can be linear, showing a straight line increase or decrease, with a steep or shallow angle, although this is rather rare. They could be exponential: start with rapid growth, reach a saturation point, and then diminish. And they can be cyclic with the curve following cycles, increasing and decreasing at different times. For example, if we were extrapolating population growth the result could be constant, that is, the population stays the same in the specified future; it could grow exponentially if the fertility rates continue to increase; it could grow slowly if there is a rapid fertility reduction; or if there is a slow fertility reduction it can grow and follow what is known as an S-curve. In general, in trend extrapolation an S-curve is seen as 'logistic growth' and the most realistic assumption.

Not all trends can be quantified, or analysed on the basis of one or two variables. And trends can be complex, particularly where they involve social or political dimensions, multiple actors and intricate interactions. In this case, you have to move to a more sophisticated technique known as 'morphological analysis'. Here, all possible parameters and their relationships, or

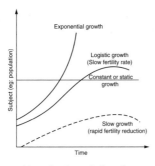

▲ Various outcomes of trend extrapolation, for example growth in population.

'configurations', are analysed. The level of complexity and the qualitative nature of the trend requires certain judgements to be made: each parameter is assigned a range of relevant 'values' or conditions. A morphological 'box' or matrix is constructed by setting the parameters against each other, and each cell in the matrix is assigned one particular value or condition from each of the parameters. What follows requires advanced mathematics and computers to analyse and study. The final product comes out in terms of probabilities.

Another commonly used method of foreseeing the future is 'age-cohort analysis'. It is based on the realization that generations of people, or 'age cohorts', who were born and who grew up in the same place during the same time span, often share the same ideas and beliefs about the world. But the ideas and beliefs about the world of different age cohorts are very different from each other. The worldview of a current age cohort in a particular place, for example, would be very different from the age cohorts who are only a decade or so younger or older than them. Think of the difference between the beat generation of the 1960s and the 'greed is good' (as Gordon Gecko declares in *Wall Street*) generation of the 1980s.

When one age cohort retires and passes political and economic power to a new age cohort with a different worldview, the world and the future change. The incoming cohorts implement different policies and programmes, and different ideas and beliefs become dominant. Age-cohort analysis compares and contrasts the outlooks of different cohorts, investigates how pre-natal, early natal and childhood experience influence the thought and behaviour of a generation, and then proceeds to ask a series of pertinent questions. What are the age groups of an organization, business, community or nation? What are the main characteristics of the age cohort in position of power and influence? What are the main characteristics of the emerging age cohort? How might things change when the dominant age group retires and a new one takes over? Such questions can be used to explore a whole array of different areas from changes in policy to economic activity to international relations and increase or decrease in crime.

A trend is a trend is a trend,

But where and when will it bend

Will it shoot to the sky,

Turn over and die,

Or asymptote off to the end.

B.C. Twiss, 1981

▲ Like vintage wine, cohorts have specific characteristics.

Age-cohort analysis tends to emphasize the fact that the future can often be cyclical. Successive age cohorts tend to recycle ideas and beliefs of the previous generation in an established pattern. In the US, for example, four cohort types have influenced the direction of the country in cyclical fashion: idealists, who have a new well-articulated vision of the future which they cannot realize in their lifetimes; reactives, who react negatively to the idealist dream; civics, who adopt the idealist goals, which by now have become weak, and try to fulfil it; and adaptives, who try to do the best they can with the old ideals but are rather cynical about the future.[1] Once the cycle has exhausted itself, new idealists emerge with a new dream and the cycle repeats itself. Other nations will have different cohort types; but all nations and communities have certain cohort types. If we know which cohort type will come to power, we can foresee what changes will emerge and anticipate the future over the horizon.

▶ Horizon scanning

'Horizon scanning', also known as 'futures scanning', is the most widely used method in government ministries and departments, local authorities, corporations and big businesses. It is normally applied to issues of technology, economy and commerce. Often used to provide evidence for strategic planning and futures thinking, horizon scanning involves screening a large body of data on a regular basis, according to certain criteria, and looking for symptoms of change. Most newspaper readers are in fact regularly involved in horizon scanning. They scan the headlines as they turn the pages of the newspaper, and then zoom in on the article that they actually want to read. After the article has been read, horizon scanning is resumed. Professional horizon scanning would involve a much higher level of attention, looking for things that are outside conventional categories, or appear to make no sense or look odd, or for issues that straddle established boundaries, in a logically structured and iterative process. The aim is to spot trends and changes in the near and medium future with the potential for positive or negative impact. The information that is scanned would not only include published sources, such as newspapers, magazines and learned and scholarly journals, but also surveys and market research (which could be specifically commissioned), the web, as well as expert opinions and Delphi polls. The information chosen for scanning proposes is specifically selected for its known richness and relevance to the criteria. Most horizon scanning processes involve five distinct steps:

(1) searching for information resources, (2) selecting information respurces to scan, (3) developing the criteria for scanning, (4) scanning, and (5) determining the appropriate action to take based on the results.

The results could identify emerging trends and developments if the signals emerging from horizon scanning are strong, clearly visible and concrete. But quite frequently the signals that emerge are weak and difficult to detect. Sometimes they are confusing and not easy to discern or analyse. Other times they are just spurious and do not indicate a true change or trend.

Weak signals are easy to dismiss as inaccurate or irrelevant. But weak signals can be very important as they provide us with a vague warning sign. It is no surprise then that a whole range of complicated methodologies have evolved to identify and make sense of weak signals.[2] One particular method to grasp the significance of a weak signal is to pass it through what is known as Ansoff's filters, named after Igor Ansoff, the Russian–American expert on strategic management. The first, surveillance filter, concerns the environment of the organization which has identified the weak signal. We need to know how this organization is changing and evolving. The second, mentality filter, involves evaluating the signal's relevance, meaning and value on the basis of a hypothesis on the potential impact of the emerging phenomenon that the signal is indicating. Finally, the third, power filter, brings the decision-makers into play: the signal is presented to the decision-makers of the organization, after it has been interpreted and suitably translated to fit both the power structure and the strategic needs of the organization. Some signals will be blocked at each stage, while others will get through. Of course, a weak signal can be rejected as spurious even after passing through all three filters, which could have serious consequences for an organization.

Weak signals are sometimes used to anticipate what in futures studies is called *wild cards*. While weak signals are small and apparently insignificant issues that point to potential changes and trends in the future, wild cards are sudden and unexpected events that have immense consequences for the future. Wild cards take everyone by surprise and happen so quickly that our social, political, economic or cultural systems cannot effectively respond to them. The leap from horse to car and typewriter to computer are examples of historic wild cards. The sudden collapse of the Soviet Union, the rapid emergence of global multimedia monopolies, the terrorist attacks on 9/11 and the 2009 collapse of the financial markets are more recent examples. A shift in the earth's axis, a comet or asteroid attack, or the emergence of super-intelligent computers are potential future wild cards. Paying due attention to weak signals can sometimes help us to anticipate wild cards in advance.

There is no easy solution for identifying weak signals. However, if a signal is repeated, if it now comes from different sources or if it is reinforced by other similar signals then there may be grounds for electing the set of signals as an important messenger of change. This clustering of signals is called 'cumulative signals'.

A variety of signals arising in different contexts elicits an exercise of 'networking of meaning' in an analogous way as the appearance of an increasing number of dead rats in different places leads the characters of Albert Camus to realize that a plague is taking hold of their city. The subtle implication also conveyed by this evocative metaphor is that as weak signals grow strong by combining with other signals, the scope for action gets narrower and narrower. That is, they develop into strong signals.

Sandro Mendonca *et al.*, 'The strategic strength of weak signal analysis', Futures 44 (3) 218–28, April 2012

▶ Global models

Both weak signals and wild cards underline the fact that future events are embedded in a web of interrelated issues and problems. Thus forecasting future events in isolation from one another fails to take into account the mutual effect of a host of interconnected issues and other possible future events. One way to overcome this shortcoming, and increase the reliability of forecasts, is to use 'cross-impact analysis'. As the name itself suggests, this method examines how relationships across and between different events would impact the resulting events. It involves identifying events that might affect a particular area of interest and then creating links between possible future events, while monitoring trends that are relevant to the interest area. The relationships between events and trends are categorized as positive or negative to each other and depicted in a 'cross-impact matrix'. A typical cross-impact matrix considers 10 to

40 events, involves calculating probabilities that events have on each other, and can be highly complex. That is why computer simulation models are frequently used in the analysis. The final result tells us which events are more likely to occur in a given time frame. The technique is widely used in industry to chart the future development of particular technologies, exploration of national futures and in the study of terrorism.

Computer simulations are often used to model reality, tackle complexity in a matrix of interactions and develop long-term forecasts. Basically, a computer model replicates real-world relationships that can be quantified and subjected to manipulation. The model can be relatively simple and predict something very specific such as flow of traffic in a junction; or it can be quite complex and sophisticated, representing ecological systems or the earth as a whole and providing forecasts of changes in the global environment. The best known is the 'global dynamic' model that became the basis for the 1972 *The Limits to Growth* report from the Club of Rome. It used population growth, food production, pollution and natural resources to examine what will happen to the world if nothing changed and things continued normally. Since then computing capacity has increased many-fold and computer models and simulations have proliferated. Their omnipresent presence can be felt in Hollywood blockbusters, such as *Avatar*, or games like *Sim Earth*. (In the American television series *Eureka*, set in a town populated by scientific geniuses, most of the residents work for 'Global Dynamics', a corporation that models everything on the globe and is overseen by the US Department of

Defense.) More usefully, weather forecasts, predictions of market trends and warnings about climate change are largely based on global models.

Climate change is not only the most pressing problem facing the globe, it is also one of the most complex, with numerous dimensions and levels of uncertainty, and requires a high level of co-ordination between countries. A special methodology has therefore been developed to study climate change: 'integrated assessment model'. It integrates knowledge from a number of different disciplines into a single framework. It is described as an 'assessment', rather than a method because it analyses uncertainties and aims to provide policy options for decision-making instead of making long-term forecasts. Supported by various UN agencies, integrated assessment modelling is now common in environmental sciences.

In futures studies, global issues are sometimes explored using a method called 'heuristic modelling', which seeks insight into a variety of possible outcomes based on a broad range of variables. Heuristic modelling, which is often used for pedagogic purposes, combines a number of futures methods as Delphi, simulation, cross-impact analysis and integrated assessment models, to explore and think about global futures. At the core of heuristic modelling is a computer simulation based on a cross-impact matrix in the form of a spreadsheet. The matrix, the principal user interface, includes such selected variables as conflict, culture, education, poverty, technology, economy, population and environment, and the self- and cross-interactions between them. The users can define and clarify the meaning of the selected variables.

'For example, conflict could be defined as the number of deaths from wars, institutional violence, crime etc. but could also include psychological stress or a propensity to violence, including the size of the military or arms races. Similarly, environment may be conceptualized as an abundance of ecological diversity depleted by demographic and economic advance, but with an intrinsic capacity for regeneration, or simply as a remaining level of mineral resources. Again, with levels of human exploitation of environment, the students can ask: is nature ours for the taking; are we the caretakers of nature; or what?'[3]

Once the variables have been clarified and quantified, data can be entered in the interactive matrix, and the model can be manipulated and 'run'. The model can be used to explore such issues as the historic relationship between technical change and economic growth, impact of current policies on the future, and various possible futures for humanity. It can project a number of futures to different time horizons. Its main aim, however, is not to produce forecasts but to increase our understanding of futures issues and possible outcomes. As a teaching tool, it is used to encourage students to think empirically about global futures.

All these methods, from forecasting, horizon scanning and cross-matrix analysis to modelling and identifying weak signals from emerging issues can be used to build alternative images of the future. Descriptions or accounts of potential or possible futures are called scenarios, which is one of the most used and abused term in the futures landscape.

Scenarios

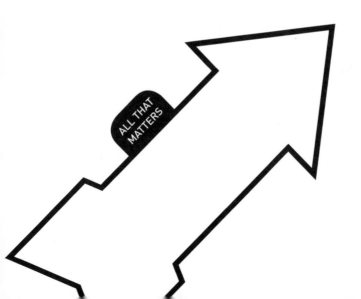

In corporations, businesses and government institutions, futures thinking is largely associated with 'scenarios'. In showbusiness, a scenario is a brief outline of a film, a play or a television series that provides the basic plot line and descriptions of main characters. In futures studies, scenarios are postulated sequences of future developments: short stories about future possibilities, if you like. On a more technical level, Herman Kahn, who is regarded as a father of scenarios, describes them as a set of hypothetical events set in the future constructed to clarify a possible chain of causal events as well as their decision points.[1] Michel Godet, the French pioneer of perspective and scenario planning, defines them as a 'coherent set of hypotheses leading from a given original situation to a future situation'.[2]

The term is usually used in the plural because it is taken for granted that there are a number of potential futures. But a range of other terms, such as thinking, planning, analysis, technique and building, are frequently added to scenarios. All these different terms, however, mean the same thing: speculating about different future outcomes to reduce uncertainty in decision-making. The purpose of scenarios is not to predict but to explore images of possible alternative futures, based on trends, emerging issues and weak signals, and identify both threats and opportunities. Scenarios are not about constructing an ideal or a preferred future, but to determine real possibilities and use them to make contingency plans. In times of uncertainty and rapid innovation and change, scenarios can be invaluable in strategic management and risk analysis. As a management tool, scenarios serve as aids to decision-makers, provide them with a context for planning and programmes, and raise the level of their knowledge about the consequences of possible actions that have to be taken in the current circumstances.

It was during a time of crisis and uncertainty in the oil market, after the emergence of OPEC in the 1970s, that scenarios first gained wide currency. The lead was taken by Shell, considered by many to be a pioneer in the field, to develop specific scenarios to cope successfully with oil stocks and other uncertainties in the market. The number of US companies using scenarios doubled within a year. By the early 1980s, over half of Fortune 1000 companies were actively using scenarios. Since then scenarios have been extensively used at corporate level and have also been applied successfully at national level.

There are several methods for generating scenarios, which can be qualitative, quantitative or a combination of both; extrapolative or normative; and can range from simple to highly sophisticated. The 'Shell approach', which is probably the most straightforward, is based on an 'intuitive logic' that involves between 5 and 15 – or sometimes more – precise steps leading to the construction of a hypothetical sequence of events. A set of key moments, or decision points, which could alter trends are identified as important for decision-making. The key moments could occur over a span of time, 5, 10 or 20 years in the future, depending on the subject or area around which the scenarios are being built. The approach combines both precise environmental factors such as demography, and qualitative factors that are more difficult to predict such as product demands, customer attitudes, economic conditions and geopolitical circumstances. An alternative approach, called the 'probabilistic modified trends method', emerged from futures work at the RAND Corporation. It combines traditional forecasting techniques, such as trend extrapolation and cross-impact analysis, to enhance scenario analysis. Both these approaches are widely used in the US.

▲ Sometimes, it is the one on its own, outside the fold, who really matters.

In contrast to the RAND and Shell approaches, the French methods for scenario construction tends to be highly mathematical and computer based. Scenarios were promoted in France by the Office for Regional Planning and Development (DATAR) during the 1960s and 1970s, and have been used extensively in public sector planning. Its leading proponent, Michel Godet, who worked at the Department of Future Studies at Conservatoire National des Arts et Metiers (CNAM), passionately promoted the belief that alternative futures can be modelled and scenarios can serve as a guiding vision to policymakers. Godet takes a very rigorous approach to building scenarios, and has complained that the term itself has been badly used and abused: 'if you had a penny for each time you used scenario', you would get very rich, but 'its scientific nuance in futures thinking has been diluted'.[3] Godet uses a form of cross-impact matrixes and 'morphological analysis' (a complex method for solving multi-dimensional, non-quantified real-world problems such as marketing or making public policy) to produce highly sophisticated and detailed scenarios. His work has been used in France to develop new individual combat weapons, estimate how insurance premiums will change in the future, explore food safety, and determine whether Paris would need a third airport in 2030.

There are numerous other methods for developing scenarios, leading to what has been described as a 'methodological chaos' of characteristics, principles and processes found in the futures and foresight literature.

Although scenarios can be developed by individuals, they are most effective when produced by groups. The group works both as a single collective and as sub-groups to analyse the degree of uncertainty and the complexity of the problem being examined, to identify key environmental forces and decision factors, the timescale in which the project is to be undertaken, the resources available, the stakeholders involved and the expected outcome. To provide alternatives it is necessary to have more than one scenario. There ought to be one that presents the worst possible case, one that presents a rosy picture, one that is probable given the current trends, one that is unlikely but important to consider, and many in between. In most cases at least four different scenarios are developed for a given issue or situation. All scenarios, whatever the techniques used in developing them, follow a set of logical steps. In their practical guide, *Scenario Thinking*, British futurists George Wright and George Cairns summarize these steps into a process involving eight stages:

Stage 1: Setting the agenda – defining the issue and process, and setting the scenario timescale;

Stage 2: Determining the driving forces – working, first, individually, and as a group;

Stage 3: Clustering the driving forces – group discussion to develop, test and name the clusters;

Stage 4: Defining the cluster outcomes – defining two extreme, but yet highly plausible, and hence highly possible, outcomes for each of the clusters over the scenario timescale;

Stage 5: Impact/uncertainty matrix – determining the key scenario factors;

Stage 6: Framing the scenarios – defining the extreme outcomes of the key factors;

Stage 7: Scoping the scenarios – building the set of broad descriptions for four scenarios;

Stage 8: Developing the scenarios – working in sub-groups to develop scenario storylines, including key events, their chronological structure, and the 'who and why' of what happens.[4]

Each stage can be developed and elaborated further. For example, in setting the scenario agenda, you can ask a series of questions: how would you describe your ideal future, what factors and events do you think will be necessary to make them happen, who will be the key players, what obstacles do you see, and so on. Or the attempts to identify driving forces can go beyond simply identifying general trends, such as changing attitudes and the emergence of new technologies, to a detailed examination of emerging issues. However, whether the process is simple or highly detailed, in order for the scenarios to be valid the analysis must be coherent, and the scenarios themselves must be logically sound, plausible, transparent and easy to recount and illustrate. In other words, they must provide a description of a credible future and an internally consistent account of how that future would unfold, tell the story of how trends might develop over time and what impact they could have.

Normally, scenarios are written in the present tense as if the future they are describing has already happened. It helps if they can portray difference vividly and boldly. Once the scenarios are completed, the real work begins. To be useful, they have to be incorporated into the decision-making process. They ought to help in developing flexible strategies and appropriate monitoring systems to navigate the uncertain future. It is here that certain limitations of scenarios become evident.

How do you know, for example, whether you have the right scenarios? The process of building scenarios, involving a balance between individual and teamwork, can lead to arbitrary scenarios themes. If different initial assumptions were made, or the make-up of the group was different, or certain driving forces were overlooked, very different scenarios could emerge. But even if you think you have the right scenarios, it is not always clear how you go from scenarios to actual decisions. There is always the temptation to bet on a single (one's favourite) scenario, rather than think in terms of multiple future possibilities. Or to take the scenarios too literally as a map or a beacon that can guide you towards a particular future.

Four scenarios for the future of the European Union: 2030

Scenario A: Enduring Crisis

Europe continues to lurch from crisis to crisis. One in three in any member country is unemployed. The euro is, and has been, on the verge of collapse for several years. The economies of many European states resemble the poorer states of Africa. But somehow the Union has managed to survive. At a demonstration in Brussels, placards read: 'Enough is Enough'; 'Bring Back Our Subsidies'; 'We want Jobs – NOW'; and, the obligatory, 'The End of the World is Nigh'.

Scenario B: United States of Europe

The President of the Federation was warmly welcomed in London. Crowds in Trafalgar Square cheered and waved USE flags as they listened to his speech. 'I can say with confidence that our Federation of fifty states is now the strongest economy in the world', he declared. The euro has replaced the dollar as the global currency, and Europe has emerged as a global superpower, with its own army and unified foreign, economic and social policies. 'There is prosperity and unity of purpose throughout this great continent of ours', he said.

Scenario C: Union Collapses

Travelling through the continent, one has to change currencies several times. The economies of Spain, Italy, Portugal, Greece and many Eastern European countries have collapsed.

There is an open economic war between Germany, France, the United Kingdom and the Scandinavian countries. The 'European Quarter' of Brussels, where the EU headquarters and European Parliament were once located, is now occupied by multinational corporations.

The dream of a European Union lies in tatters.

Scenario D: Balkanized Europe

It started as a chain reaction. The declaration of independence by Catalonia was followed, almost immediately, by the Basque Country and Andalusia in Spain. A year later, Scotland broke away from the United Kingdom, and Sicily from Italy. Today, we have no fewer than 60 nations in Europe, many so small that they can be hardly described as a viable 'independent states'. Yet, they have managed to survive, and some have even thrived.

There are various techniques to overcome some of these limitations. For example, to ensure that participants in the scenario-building process function as a viable and coherent group, Godet suggests that you should stimulate the imagination, reduce inconsistency, create a common language among participants, structure the collective thinking process and encourage participants to learn from each other. But no matter how rigorous the process on which they are based, scenarios should not be seen as 'right' or 'wrong'; rather, they should be judged on the basis of range of possible and appropriate futures they delineate. As such, they are an excellent tool for collective learning, questioning time-held assumptions, and grappling with uncertainty. They can certainly be used to produce contingency plans, but to be more effective as a decision-making tool, they have to be integrated with other tools for anticipating the future. Scenario planning should be seen as just one component among many of managing change in uncertain and turbulent times.

In building scenarios it is often useful to ask 'what if' questions. What if this driving force melts into thin air? Or, what if a key variable changes? What effect will it have on other driving forces and the overall scenarios? In futures studies, a broad range of 'what if' questions have been used for decades to think about and explore future developments. What if genetic engineering made human reproduction redundant? What if a terminator-like robot was actually developed by the US military? What if Brazil or Mexico became the sole superpower? What if we could reverse the ageing process? Such 'what if' questions encourage you to think creatively and differently about future possibilities, imagine alternative futures and, more importantly, take you outside current realities and dominant modes of thought. 'What if' questions can also be used to challenge your assumptions and biases about the future, address issues of change, bring choices and options into sharper focus and create new ideas and categories of thought. They can be flippant, like the question Livvy asks her husband Norman, in Isaac Asimov's story 'What if': 'what if fish had wings and all of them flew to the top of the mountains? What would we have to eat on Fridays then?' Or they can be serious. Either way they stick in your mind.

What if you could relocate yourself in a future you desire?

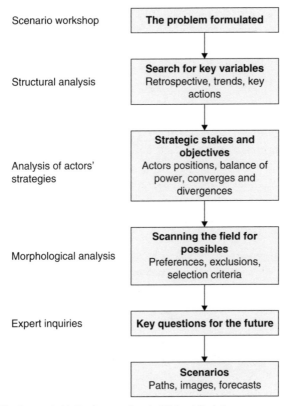

Scenario workshop	**The problem formulated**
Structural analysis	**Search for key variables** Retrospective, trends, key actions
Analysis of actors' strategies	**Strategic stakes and objectives** Actors positions, balance of power, converges and divergences
Morphological analysis	**Scanning the field for possibles** Preferences, exclusions, selection criteria
Expert inquiries	**Key questions for the future**
	Scenarios Paths, images, forecasts

▲ The Scenario Method, according to Michael Godet.

Looking backwards

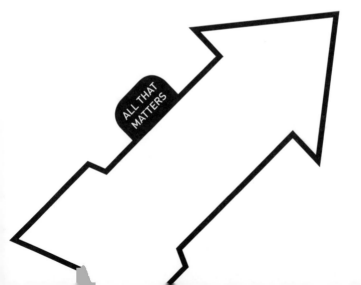

ALL THAT MATTERS

Before you can relocate to your desired future, you need to have a good idea of the actual future you desire. In other words, you need to have a vision of your future. Most of us have a vision of a future society, although few of us actually articulate it or think about it seriously. Many corporations and companies have a 'vision' of their business but it is limited to their future 'projects' and producing 'new and improved' products. Those who do have a concrete vision tend to be ideologues who think, like the eponymous hero of Voltaire's *Candide*, that their vision is the best vision in this best of all possible worlds and can be imposed uniformly upon one and all.

▲ Present times are shaped by our metaphors and perceptions of future times.

In futures studies, visions play a specific role in a method called 'backcasting'. The purpose of backcasting is to provide 'policy makers and an interested general public with images of the future as a background for opinion forming and decisions' in the hope that 'new knowledge and new ideas may lead to the identification of some entirely new options'.[1] Unlike forecasting, which analyses trends and looks towards the future, backcasting uses normative future visions to provide the necessary strategy for its realizations. Instead of forecasting, the future is 'backcast'. It is important to realize the distinctions between forecasting and backcasting: 'backcasting is set in a context of discovery whereas forecasting is set in one of justification; backcasting is shaped by purpose whereas forecasting is shaped by causality; and the fundamentals of backcasting are uncertainty and indeterminacy whereas for forecasting they are determinism and predictability'.[2] As such, backcasting allows us to move away from current trends and create desirable futures that are fundamentally different from the current conditions. Backcasting is particularly useful and comes on its own when trend analysis and long-term forecasts indicate that goals and targets cannot be met within the stipulated time, and you need solutions that actually break trends. It has become an essential tool for urban planning, imagining the futures of cities, management of resources such as water and energy, transport development and exploring issues of sustainability.

As in other methods in futures studies, there are a number of approaches to backcasting. Some are overtly normative and goal- and target-oriented. One particular method, known as 'The Natural Step', aims at tackling complexity and developing techniques for safeguarding biodiversity and ecosystems; it has been used extensively in Sweden and Canada. Another method, called STD after the Dutch government programme for Sustainable Technology Development where it was developed, involves broad stakeholder participation, emphasizes creativity to break out of conventional notions and mindsets, and explores time horizons of 50 years and beyond. But all methods of backcasting follow a standard procedure, which involves five stages: (1) setting the agenda and identifying stakeholders; (2) construction of sustainable future visions; (3) backcasting; (4) elaboration, analysis and defining follow-up and (action) agenda; and (5) marshalling commitment to change.

Any meaningful backcasting exercise must involve a broad range of stakeholders. In the case of institutions a whole range of employees, from the Board to the ground floor, have to be involved. Communities and cities have to include actors from different societal groups as well as government, companies, public interest groups, experts and academics, both in developing a shared vision and in doing the reverse planning. The backcasting carried out at Göteborg, Sweden, for example, involved most of the institutions of the city, including the university, utility companies, public municipal and regional companies, as well as the citizens of the city. Moreover, there should be a clear agenda for the exercise: what is it looking at?

'Project Göteborg 2050', which aims to transform Göteborg into a sustainable city, looked at urban design, food, recycling, transportation and solar energy – and developed elaborate long-term plans for each of them.[3] But backcasting need not be so elaborate – it can be undertaken, just as effectively, by smaller communities and focused on specifics such as employment or regeneration of a local area.

Although it is conventional to describe the procedure as distinctive linear steps, the process can be iterative. It may become necessary to go back to the visions to refine them, or return to the backcasting stage for further elaboration. Some stakeholders may leave, and others may step in.

▶ Visions

The most difficult aspect of backcasting is developing a vision. All of us have our own vision. And we expect others to have their vision. But in a backcasting, we need a shared vision that leads to successful action. This may be a relatively easy exercise for a business organization, where the issue is focused on particular products or services. For organizations, visions are basically a leadership tool; a visionary business leader not only inspires their workforce but provides a sense of direction for the organization. Their vision could be linked to strategic planning. But developing visions for communities, cities or large social institutions is on a different order of scale. We have to involve a large group of diverse actors who have to be motivated to produce a collective conception of what the ideal future could or should look like.

▲ Visions open new windows of potential and possibility.

Like scenario work, visioning is a collective endeavour. But visions are somewhat different from scenarios. Scenarios can be regarded as futures of the head: they allow us to explore our assumptions about possibilities; while visions are futures for the heart, giving us a voice to articulate our most deeply felt values and goals.[4] In contrast to scenarios, which have to be concrete, visions can be bold and idealistic and express our hopes and aspirations. Visions can be qualitative as well as quantitative. They have to be located in a clearly defined time horizon: a vision of society, a city, a community or something more specific, 20, 30 or more years from now.

Visions describe future history that we desire as individuals and communities. Visions inspire and encourage people to act. In futures studies, a vision is defined as an imagined representation of a desired future and visioning is seen as a process of creating a series of images of the future that are both real and compelling. Visions stimulate positive values and actions and guide the choices and behaviour of individuals and collectives towards a desired future. A vision is like a magnet that pulls the present towards an imagined future and like a compass, a vision can indicate the future direction towards which we wish to travel.

But not all participants in a backcasting exercise will wish to travel in the same direction. In any given group, there will be men and women, people with different ethnicities, cultures and backgrounds. They will all have different hopes and aspirations for the future and therefore different visions. Even men and women from the same cultural background could have distinctively different visions. Indeed, feminist futurists have argued that men tend to have grand visions focused on political power and technological advancement, while women lean towards human relationships, envision future societies free of patriarchy where the marginalized and the powerless are brought to the centre from the periphery. The famous American futurist, Elise Boulding, has pointed out that there is a particular quality to the way women think about the future which sets them apart from the conventional male manipulative and adversarial way men talk about the future;[5] and Eleonora Masini argues that women are more capable of understanding 'incipient changes' by virtue of the fact that they have not been builders of the dominant system. They can cope more easily with complex situations where emotion and intuition are as important as the intellect. A good example of the women's vision is summed up by the title of the American futurist Hazel Henderson's famous 1996 book *Building a win-win world: Life beyond global economic warfare.*[6]

'Just do it'

In backcasting, we are not too concerned with visions of personal development. If you are seeking meaning in your life, or ways to enlighten yourself, or want to instil self-belief so you can 'achieve anything', it is probably better to consult a self-help manual. Visioning is about negotiating and constructing positive visions of the future, not about promoting the idea that good citizens can best look after themselves by denying social relations. It is about only those visions that make an explicit or implicit claim about the future.

There will, of course, be other differences. Some would argue for a humanistic vision, a society built on universal values with an accent on justice and equity. The Indian futurist and social activist Nandini Joshi, for example, envisions the future of the world community 'not in the huge, crowded, cumbersome, crime-threatened cities, overridden with unemployment and inflation' but in 'lustrous, flourishing, free villages overflowing with useful goods, professions, intelligence and arts'.[7] Others would opt for a religious vision, where the Hereafter is seen as more important than the material world. Still others would project ideological visions, translated into political programmes. Ethnic and cultural differences between participants in a visioning exercise could produce even more radically diverse visions. Thus, any visioning exercise that involves a diverse group or community would produce a number of conflicting visions. A great deal of negotiation is thus required between contesting visions to produce a vision that has overall legitimacy and can provide a common ground for programmes and joint action to realize the vision.

Moreover, to be meaningful, visions have to be based on physical reality and must not be utopian and therefore unrealizable. Utopias can be particularly hazardous in visioning. If they are based on current values and norms, there is a strong possibility that they could turn into nightmares. To avoid this trap we need to step out of our current values and concerns, shake off the influences that dominate our thoughts and actions, and take an imaginative leap. In particular, we need three distinctive types of imagination: logical imagination that is used to show the absurdity of current trends and contests conventional views; critical imagination that probes deeper 'searching for structural weaknesses in the existing state of affairs and thereby creating the context for alternative futures'; and creative imagination that 'strikes out on a completely new course, breaking radically with prevalent concepts'.[8] Visions have to take full account of diversity and ennoble people as well as stimulate their imagination.

Once a vision that can provide a shared platform has been developed we can move to backcasting. The process of backcasting involves asking a series of time-related questions. We start from the future in which the vision is located, and work backwards. If the vision, for example, is a vision of a city in 2040, we ask: what must happen in the city in 2039 for the vision to be realized in 2040? What must happen in 2038 to trigger the relevant, desired events for 2039? What must happen in 2037 to ensure that what we want to happen in 2038 happens? These fundamental questions are asked systematically, year after year, right back to the present time. Of course, we do not have to work in single years. We could backcast in two-, three- or five-year periods. The aim is to work backwards to identify milestones that must occur at each juncture, and identify the steps that need to be taken to achieve each milestone. A timeline of milestones can thus be created linking the present to the vision and polices, programmes and actions needed to achieve the milestones can be developed. The end product is a detailed plan that could be used to move forward from the present, step by step, moving from milestone to milestone, towards the desired vision. The quality of backcasting, and the eventual plan, depends on how carefully the conditions for attainment are defined at each particular stage.

In backcasting we start with a vision, work backwards from the vision to identify milestones, moving stage by stage towards the present where we can take the first steps to realize the vision.

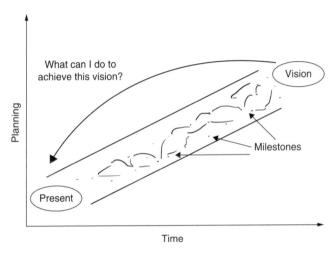

▲ The Backcasting Process.

As a planning methodology, backcasting is particularly useful when current trends are seen as problematic, when problems are just too complex and current solutions make no sense, or when you need to galvanize a group, a community or a city to shape a desired future. It can be very empowering for individuals as it brings the future right to the present moment. All successful visioning and backcasting exercises end with one straightforward question: what do I do today to achieve this vision?

Looking in all directions

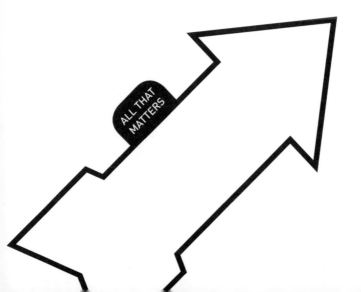

ALL THAT MATTERS

So far we have ignored the 'I', or the personal, individual dimension of discovering futures. It can be argued that if we leave our subjective considerations from futures work, and simply concentrate on the objective world and what can be measured, we are overlooking a great deal of what makes us human. More holistic and rounded explorations of alternative futures ought to include our interior, subjective concerns. This is particularly so given that futures exploration, by definition, is an inter-, multi- and trans-disciplinary activity. Two approaches have emerged over the last decade that attempt to be more inclusive, and concentrate on both the subjective as well as the cultural dimensions of thinking about the future: 'integral futures' and 'causal layered analysis'.

The 'integral' in integral futures refers to a combined multi-dimensional analysis which includes as many viewpoints and outlooks as possible. The dictionary definition of integral is something that is 'essential or necessary for completeness'; integral futures suggests that a futures inquiry is not complete if it does not take a whole range of subjective perspectives into consideration. To be integral, we must accept all 'truths' as equally valid and acknowledge the validity of different ways of knowing across disciplines, cultures and worldviews.

The approach itself is rather simple, although the analysis can be sophisticated and quite complex. Integral futures is based on the thesis that there are four fundamental perspectives, like the four fundamental forces of nature, that describe 'reality' and must be considered in any futures work: subjective, intersubjective (social), objective and interobjective (cultural). The perspectives, the ways of knowing, being and doing, are represented in a four quadrants model, each quadrant dedicated to a particular perspective. The quadrants personify the interior/exterior world of individuals/collectives, are intrinsically linked to each other and evolve in unison.

Interior	Exterior	
Subjective 'I'	Objective 'It'	
		Individual
		Collective
Cultural 'We'	Social 'Its'	

▲ The Integral Futures Quadrant.

The upper left quadrant represents the subjective perspective, the interior world of an individual, concerned with motivation, values, aspirations, goals, hopes, fears and meaning of life. It is the realm of the 'I'. The upper right quadrant represents the objective perspective, the exterior world of an individual, concerned with people's outward behaviour such as relationships, consumption patterns, political allegiances and professional concerns. It is about 'it' – the object out there. The lower left quadrant represents the intersubjective or cultural perspectives, the interior world, of a collective; the meaning they share as a community, expressed as culture, tradition and customs. Here the language of 'we' or 'us' is prominent. The lower right quadrant represents the intersubjective or social perspective, the exterior world of the collective, which in fact is the physical world of systems, institutions and structures – the combined 'its'. Here, the concerns of the collective can be measured objectively in changes in natural or constructed environment.

Each quadrant personifies a particular type of 'truth' that relates to a particular type of knowledge enclosed within the quadrant. For example, the knowledge in the upper right quadrant is observable and empirical, but the knowledge in the upper left quadrant is interpretative and invisible. It is the domain of the 'I'; the only person who can 'know' or has this knowledge is the individual. Others must engage with the individual's consciousness to appreciate or even get a glimpse of this knowledge. But both types of knowledge are equally valid and provide different perspectives on reality or a given context. Both perspectives are essential or necessary for completeness, for understanding the full picture. Physicist and futurist Joseph Voros writes that

Central to this approach to futures is the role of human consciousness – images of the future require a consciousness in which to be held, so we cannot reasonably study the content of images of the future without also understanding the container. What we see going on 'out there' in the world is, in large part, conditioned by what is going on 'in here' in our minds. Our perspective creates our perception of reality. In other words, ontology and epistemology – being and knowing, existing and thinking – are merely two sides of the same coin. Integral Futures takes this simple but profound recognition as central to its programme for understanding how the past was laid down, how the present has come to be, and what futures may yet come to pass.[1]

A great deal of futures research and analysis tends to be reductive. It concentrates on the exterior aspects and sees reality as monochromatic. Integral futures sidesteps reduction in favour of a more all-inclusive and rounded vision of futures. One would not expect an approach that emphasizes a plurality of perspectives to be confined to a single tool or method. So integral futures uses all the methods we examined in previous chapters as well as many intuitive and spiritual techniques. But the accent in integral futures is always on bringing the 'interior collective' (society) and the 'interior individual' (the unique world of each person) domains together. The end result, claims Australian futurist Richard Slaughter, who developed the integral futures approach, can provide:

a balancing of inner and outer perspectives;

multiple and yet systematic views of our species' history and development;

access to the dynamics of social construction, innovation and 'deep design';

aspects of the 'deep structures' of this and more advanced civilizations;

a new focus on the whole spectrum of developmental options for practitioners and others (not merely their cognitive abilities); and

new and renewed methodologies and approaches.[2]

▶ Causal layered analysis

Causal layered analysis, or CLA for short, concerns itself with exposing the underlying assumptions of futures thinking. In contrast to trend analysis, horizon scanning, scenarios and backcasting, which focus on the horizontal and spatial aspects of futures, CLA looks at the vertical dimensions, perceived as 'layers'. The overall objective of the method is to highlight the parochial and brittle nature of current social practices so they are not unconsciously projected into the future as universal truths and practices. CLA seeks to 'undefine' the future in an attempt to ensure that it is not taken as *a priori* given, that trend and projections are not taken for granted, that non-western cultures, epistemologies and modes of being are appropriately represented, and a wide range of metaphors and images are used to think creatively about potential alternatives.

Developed by the Pakistani/Australian futurist Sohail Inayatullah, CLA involves four layers of analysis: the litany, social causes, discourse/worldview and metaphor/myth. The litany is simply the problem, event, trend or whatever that is the subject of the futures inquiry. It could, for example, be unemployment in a community, the ecological problems of the planet or traffic congestion in a city. The standard solutions to these problems come with certain basic assumptions. For example, to reduce congestion we add extra lanes or build more roads. But rather than solving the problems, the conventional approach actually makes the problem worse. CLA focuses our attention on the proposed solutions to interrogate them, question the rulebook on which they are based, and move away from the standard knowledge structure, or paradigm, within which problems are framed and solutions are proposed.

The second layer, social causes, broadens the analysis and brings the context into play. Both problems and their solutions are perceived within economic, social, cultural, historical or political contexts. Thus, unemployment in a community would be seen as an economic issue, the ecological problems as a result of industrial pollution and congestion as a product of urbanization, rapid development that puts more cars on the road and economic growth. A potential solution to congestion would be to switch from an industrial to an information economy. CLA emphasises that the context (economic, social or political) is itself a problem: it not only causes or mediates the issue, such as unemployment and road congestion, but actually constitutes it. Indeed, the context, as well as the knowledge system developed to understand and control the context, are delinquents: they are in need of serious analytical chastisement.

Once both the problem and its context have been problematized, the analysis moves on to examine the overall structure that sustains and legitimizes both: the third level. The technique is borrowed from cultural studies where it is called discourse analysis. A discourse is a strongly bounded area of social and cultural knowledge, a system of assumptions, statements, disciplines and ideas. We understand the world through discourses. Indeed, some critical theorists have argued that the world is not simply 'there' to be understood and appreciated; rather, it is through discourses that the world is brought into being. Perhaps the most famous example of a discourse is Orientalism, the historical construction of eastern cultures as alien and exotic objects of western scrutiny in scholarship, art and literature. Orientalism has served as a key feature of western attitudes and writings about the Orient from the eighteenth century to today. It promotes a sense of fundamental difference between the West – 'us' – and the East – 'them'. It is not just a way of knowing the Orient but also a way of maintaining power over it.[3]

Discourse analysis examines the power relationships that are created by discourses in an attempt to give voice to those who have been marginalized from and within the discourse. In CLA, the discourse layer is analysed in two forms. First, the structures of the discourses, where the litany and social causes are located, are interrogated. So in our example of traffic congestion, we need to look at the discourses of city planning, discourses that promote urbanization, discourses that favour private transport over public transport and so on. The aim is to understand how the discourse that we use to appreciate and frame the problem is actually complicit in creating the problem in the first place. Second, CLA sees futures studies as a discourse; hence any solutions offered from the conventional perspective of forecasts, scenarios and other methods need to be examined from the viewpoint of power. Here, the language of futures thinking is just as important as the specific type of knowledge about the future it seeks to promote. Language is much more than simply a mode of communication but is closely related to the social and cultural needs that it is required to serve. Far from being symbolic, it is actually constitutive of reality.

The analysis becomes deeper and deeper as we move towards the final layer: metaphor. This layer seeks to deconstruct our creative processes in thinking about the future. Metaphors create meaning and draw our attention to some similarity that exists between two things. But they may also create a new similarity, and hence a new meaning. While requiring a certain level of creativity, metaphors do not emerge from nothing; they are, in fact, deeply embedded in our unconscious myths. Notice how advertising uses visual metaphors created out of known cultural myths to engage us and encourage us to buy the product that is being sold. Once the metaphor is connected to the myth, we tend to react automatically. To get away from gut, emotional reactions, we need to decode metaphors actively and imaginatively. CLA directs our attention towards the metaphors used to describe the future and question their validity, and expose the myths on which they are based. The solutions to congested roads, for example, are based on the myths that more (lanes) or bigger (highways) are the solution, or that the standard (western) solutions to congestion are best. Perhaps we can find more viable solutions by directing our attention to different, non-western metaphors.

CLA is not a linear exercise. It requires us to move up and down the levels a number of times. We need to appreciate that behind an empirical problem (the litany), there is a social and cultural context, and behind the context there is a discourse and a worldview which themselves are based on myths. CLA aims to expose current power relationships, and encourages using categories of knowledge and thought from other cultures and civilizations. The goal, writes Inayatullah, is to make the present distant by filtering it through historical, cultural and civilizational filters, so it appears less right, less remarkable.

'This allows the spaces of reality to loosen and the new possibilities, ideas and structures, to emerge. The issue is less what is the truth but how truth functions in particular policy settings, how truth is evoked, who evokes it, how it circulates, and who gains and loses by particular nominations of what is true, real and significant.'[4]

The questions we constantly ask as we move up and down the layers are: which interpretations of the past are valorized? What histories make the present problematic? How does the ordering of knowledge differ across civilization, gender and worldviews? Who is seen as the 'Other', inalienably different from 'us'? And which vision of the future is used to maintain the present?

Both CLA and integral futures have evolved within the critical futures tradition. They are sometimes described as 'methods' but they are approaches, rather than methods, that provide a framework for analysing and critiquing various theories, methods and ways of exploring futures. Both aim to broaden the categories of futures thinking, bring non-western cultures and epistemologies into the frame, and thus open up spaces for genuine transformation, alternatives and positive visions.

Utopias

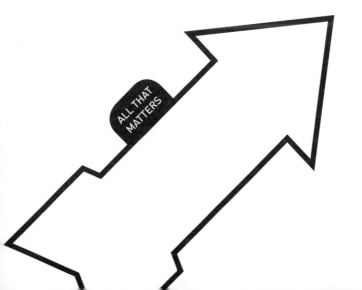

ALL THAT MATTERS

Visions of a good society are present in the narrative traditions of most cultures. As we saw in Chapter 3, philosophers, thinkers and visionaries have imagined a better future for humanity throughout history. Some of these visions have been expressed in optimistic terms, such as Thomas More's *Utopia* or Ernest Callenbach's noted 1975 novel *Ecotopia*, while others have been pessimistic, or dystopian, like George Orwell's *Nineteen Eighty-Four* or Aldous Huxley's 1932 work *Brave New World*. Either way they shine a light on an image of a possible future.

▲ Cityscapes: an arena of our anxieties with out-of-control technologies.

Literally, a *utopia* is an imagined place where everything is perfect; so perfect, in fact, that in Greek the word means 'no place'. The term was fabricated by More: it served both as the name of the island on which the story was set as well as the title of the novel. More combined the Greek words 'outopia' and 'eutopia' meaning simultaneously 'another place' and 'no place'. It is 'no place' in the sense that it does not exist and is purely imagined, but is also 'another place' in that it can possibly exist. This contradiction is important: it emphasizes the fact that utopias are an imagined construction and not a blueprint for an idealized society.

Utopias can be seen as a scheme of pure, *a priori* imagination poured into ethics, politics and aesthetics. As a representation of a future possibility, utopias have a tremendous hold on the present. Their creative and destructive potential lies in the present – the context that has produced them and in which they are rooted. In general, utopias deal with broad matters: how we can advance society, how social relations can be improved, what a just and equitable polity would look like. Their function is to inspire people to think of better worlds as well as to critique the existing world. The more detailed and concrete the utopia, the more likely it is to stimulate reflections on the shortcomings of our current situation and motivate us to struggle for a better future.

Utopias and utopian thought have been disparaged by political thinkers such as Karl Popper and Karl Mannheim. Popper declared political utopias to be dangerous, and associated them with fascist movements. Mannheim argued that utopias are illusions and paralyse every desire to change things. The concern is based on a simple observation: utopia as ideology is a totality. When ideological utopias acquire political power they become a totalitarian whole.

But utopian desires also improve our understanding of how people perceive the future, and utopias serve as useful tools for improving our understanding of future landscapes. Virtually all notions of sustainability are utopian in nature. While not all scenarios and visions are utopian, many envision a utopian world. Even some corporations have utopian visions of themselves.

To be useful to futures studies, utopias need to be open and pluralistic. One should be able to enter as well as leave a utopia. 'A utopia must show some capacity,' the noted Indian psychologist and futurist Ashis Nandy has argued, 'to liberate the utopian from its own straitjacket.' They should be open to criticism – from other visions and utopias. They cannot claim 'a monopoly on compassion and social realism' or presume to hold 'the final key to social ethics and experience'.[1]

To be open, self-critical and pluralistic, it is sometimes argued, utopias have to be humanist and secular. For example, Indian sociologist Krishan Kumar has suggested that rational and universal utopias must be totally devoid of belief.[2] But this argument constructs secularism itself as a totality by privileging it over all other worldviews. It also assumes that belief-based ideals cannot be universal or that religious people cannot be rational. It is precisely the kind of thought that both integral futures and causal layered analysis seek to expose and dethrone.

Utopias can be universal and perfectly rational and based on religious and spiritual sentiments. Muslim utopias, for example, are explicitly based on religious ideas. *The Perfect City* by the ninth-century philosopher al-Farabi,[3] *Hayy ibn Yaqzan*, the philosophical novel by the twelfth-century Andalusian thinker Ibn Tufail[4] or *Awaj bin Anfaq*, written by the thirteenth-century physician and astronomer al-Qazwini,[5] all offer a universal vision of human betterment based on religious thought. Indeed, *Hayy ibn Yaqzan* is both a defence of rationality as well as a utopian vision of a better society. In *Awaj bin Anfaq*, published around 1250, a man from a distant planet arrives on earth and is intrigued by human behaviour. The objective of the narrative, considered the first proper science fiction novel in history, is to examine universal aspirations for building a just society. More recently, in Naguib Mahfouz's *The Journey of Ibn Fattouma*[6] the protagonist, looking for his lost wife and son, spends time in two distinct religious utopias, one where freedom is valued above all and one where justice reigns supreme. The Judeo-Christian tradition too is based on religious notions of utopias as outlined by German Marxist philosopher Ernst Bloch in his celebrated work *The Principle of Hope*.[7]

Indeed, hope is the essence of utopias. Most UN declarations on such issues as eradicating poverty or building a humane, equitable and sustainable world for all contain strong elements of utopian ideals. That is why utopian thought plays an important part in futures studies. Visions of the future often have strong elements of utopian thought. Dutch futurist Ruud van der Helm has suggested that utopian visions and scenarios fulfil four basic criteria: 'they are *holistic* descriptions of a *universal society*, in which life and nature are completely under *human control*, and which *contrast strongly* with (i.e. is infinitely better than) the current society'. The imagined future society should not simply be an abstract ideal; rather it should provide us with a picture of a fully operational society. In general, the principles, institutions and organizations of this 'universal' society are based on a specific moral understanding. That is, 'every utopia is based on certain notions of right and wrong, light and darkness, and ugly and beautiful'.[8]

Moreover, utopias need not be limited to creative fiction. They can be expressed in a variety of forms: as a scientific theory or a philosophical principle, as an elaborate plan for an ecological city, or as a film such as *Avatar* (2009). Utopias can be all-inclusive, or can simply concentrate on a particular aspect of social or technological landscape.

▲ The future as envisioned in the film *Blade Runner*.

The most obvious ubiquitous images of the future are provided by science fiction, particularly science fiction cinema. While science fiction and futures explorations immerse the participant (the reader of a science fiction novel, the viewer of a film, members of a futures workshop, the forecasters, the researchers imagining alternatives) in an imagined future, there are notable differences. Science fiction tends to be dystopian.

Think of the Los Angeles of *Blade Runner* (1982), or the world of *The Terminator* (1984) or *Loopers* (2012), or the alien landscape of *Prometheus* (2012). Who would want to live in such worlds? Futures visions, on the other hand, aim both to imagine and create worlds where all of us want to live. Science fiction is often intended as a warning; it represents a possible future if things stay as they are and trends continue. Futures analysis attempts to break out of the straitjacket of trends, encourage the notion that we can do something about the future, and generally steer people away from doom and gloom.

Some notable Hollywood science fiction films

Metropolis (1927)

Things to Come (1936)

War of the Worlds (1953 and 2005)

Invasion of the Body Snatchers (1956)

On the Beach (1959)

Failsafe (1964)

The Omega Man (1971)

Rollerball (1975)

Mad Max (1979)

Alien (1979)

Blade Runner (1982)

The Day After (1983)

The Terminator (1984)

RoboCop (1987)

Running Man (1987)

Total Recall (1990)

Terminator 2 (1991)

Demolition Man (1993)

Twelve Monkeys (1995)

Independence Day (1996)

The Fifth Element (1997)

Gattaca (1997)

Starship Troopers (1997)

Deep Impact (1998)

Armageddon (1998)	*Sunshine* (2007)
The Matrix (1999)	*WALL-E* (2008)
AI: Artificial Intelligence (2001)	*Star Trek* (2009)
Minority Report (2002)	*Avatar* (2009)
I am Legend (2007)	*Loopers* (2012)

Science fiction is defined as a genre 'whose necessary and sufficient conditions are the presence and interaction of estrangement and cognition, and whose formal device is an imaginative framework alternative to the author's empirical environment'.[9] The world of science fiction is always estranged, and while the images of the future it provides may differ from the 'author's empirical world', the galaxy far, far away is always based on current fears and anxieties, the conundrum of western civilization. While the speculative imagination of science fiction complements futures studies, approaches to the future, it also employs, as I have noted elsewhere, 'particular constellations of Western thought and history and projects these Western perspectives on a pan-galactic scale. Science fiction re-inscribes Earth history, as experienced and understood by the West, across space and time.'[10] The future that science fiction offers is a populist dissention of the psyche of western civilization, its history, and its preoccupations projected into the future. That is why most science fiction concerns itself with the impact of technology.

Consider, for example, the work of H.G. Wells, the father of modern science fiction, who, as we saw in Chapter 4, coined the term 'foresight'. Wells often starts with an imaginary society based on a particular kind of advanced technology and ruled by scientists, technologists and managers of good or evil tendencies. The advanced industrial society of the 1910 novel, *When the Sleeper Wakes*, for example, is ruled by aviators and engineers.[11] The miserable and exploited workers rise up against the ruling class and their ruthless leader Ostrog and battle the 'aeroplanes' to death. A blend of Marx and technology, the novel's conclusion is that the modern, technological world has to be ruled by a small minority of technocratic elite. Indeed, in most contemporary science fiction films we find a small technocratic elite, often presented as 'The Corporation', hellbent on world domination. In science fiction, the utopian ideal is not a dream of a perfect future but the repression of plurality and free will which is often achieved by forcing human behaviour to conform to the laws of technology. In the 1997 film *Gattaca*, for example, this is achieved through the manipulation of genetic code; in *Minority Report*, which came out in 2002, the goal is realized by eradicating crime through predictive technology. Human beings have to conform to the logic of technology. Contemporary science fiction cinema offers little else but dystopian and apocalyptic visions.

In contrast to science fiction, futures studies categorically state: technology is not destiny.

However, dystopias can still be useful, not least in juxtaposing optimistic futures visions with those depicting the anxieties associated with runaway technology and other fetishes of modern and postmodern culture. In particular, the images of future cities in science fiction films, such as *Metropolis* (1927), *Blade Runner* (1982) and *The Matrix*

▲ An image from Fritz Lang's vision of the future, *Metropolis*.

(1999) have been used in research on urban futures. The abstract imaginary cities of these films extrapolate the same problems that haunt the geography of blighted communities, development plans and perpendicular metropolises. Both the 'cities of imagination' in science fiction and urban planning grapple with the estrangement, angst and isolation of urban life. Both in their particular way seek to find meaning and a sense of direction in megacities of terrifying urban landscapes. Both are a form of storytelling. That is why researchers have been able to highlight the common themes found in all urban speculations, whether they come from architecture, urban planning, development projects, regeneration schemes or science fiction novels and films:

▶ the conflict between utopian and dystopian potentials;

▶ the alienation produced in subjects in and by built environments;

▶ the relationship between built environments and nature;

▶ the effects of a centralization of oppressive or controlling power upon individual freedoms;

▶ relations between space and time; and

▶ the role of technology in future and futuristic visions of the metropolis and urban life.[12]

Urban planning uses science fiction's images of future cities as a reflection of our current concerns – which is what science fiction is all about. What it explores, and has always explored, is interior and human: the aliens are us.

Beyond utopias and dystopias, it all boils down to what we, as individuals and communities, are going to do about shaping more desirable, viable and pluralistic futures for all.

10

Shaping community futures

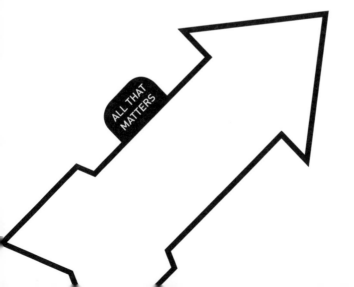

ALL THAT
MATTERS

We need some optimism to imagine and reimagine positive visions of fairer and more just futures. However, given that utopias have lost their lure, largely because they have turned out to be authoritarian undertakings, what can we do beyond hope, as individuals and communities, and work practically to shape the future we desire? Can we use the tools of futures studies to empower ourselves?

Most people feel powerless in the face of rapid change. Everyday life is too problematic and complex to think about the future. This feeling of helplessness is perhaps the most important constraint in imaging more viable and fruitful futures. Yet paradoxically, only through imagining more positive futures can we overcome our sense of helplessness. By fostering future imagination, by creating positive, shared visions of future possibilities, by identifying what is plausible and possible, we open up the arena of what could be, what ought to be, and hence motivate ourselves to engage in transformational processes.

The methods of exploring the future have been successfully used by communities and organizations to amplify their strength, motivate people to come together and create better futures, or to make complex issues more comprehensible to lay persons. Take something as complex as climate change. The science is too sophisticated for most people to understand, and is highly contested. So climate change looks difficult and remote. Yet, simply by structuring scientific climate change information into coherent scenarios, it can be made 'real', understandable and meaningful to most people. Scenarios make climate change choices more explicit, delineate possible short-term and long-term choices, and make it applicable at the community level. When such scenarios are framed with local input, and use local metaphors, they motivate local people to act.

Indeed, scenarios have served as useful instruments in urban planning, where input from local communities is essential. The process which actively involves a community in exploring and shaping the future of its urban environment is known as participatory scenario planning. While conventional planning allows the local communities nothing more than simply commenting on already developed plans, a participatory scenario planning process provides the public with an opportunity to affect the future direction of development in their communities. The shift is radical: away from a future already decided elsewhere to a vision of a more sustainable future desired by the community itself.

A good example of participatory scenario planning is provided by a project known as 'Reality Check', undertaken in the Washington Metropolitan region and the State of Maryland during 2005. For the purpose of the project, the state was divided into four regions, and the community was invited to participate in envisioning the future of their region. The facts, trends, constraints and issues were identified and derived by the community itself. The plausible futures based on current trends were compared and contrasted with the range of desired futures produced by the community. And indicators were developed so that scenarios that emerged from citizens' visioning processes can be evaluated to determine their impact on quantifiable measures of sustainable development.

All this makes the exercise appear a bit daunting. Yet it consisted simply of 'visioning days' where members of local communities were invited to take part in a day-long exercise.

The exercise used blocks of four different colours to represent the growth projections for each region: blue blocks represented jobs; white blocks represented the top 80 per cent of new housing units in the region based on price; yellow blocks represented the bottom 20 per cent of new housing based on price, essentially a stand-in for non-subsidized affordable housing; and, black blocks represented lower density housing development that could be exchanged for higher density white blocks at a ratio of 4:1. Again, each table was given a box with exactly enough coloured blocks to represent the total growth projected to come to the region. Since the outputs varied by tables and regions, after all the exercises were completed, a method was devised to aggregate everything into a single, state-wide scenario. For each region, all the tables were averaged to create a final, aggregate regional scenario. All the regional scenarios were finally joined and the resulting state-wide grid was named the Reality Check scenario.[1]

But this was not the end of the process. The participants were presented with the outcomes of each table, an aggregate vision for the region and a compilation of guiding principles – this time with two additional scenarios. One represented 'business as usual', while in the other, development occurred to fill up the entire existing capacity, without regard to sustainability or anything else. The participants could now compare their own visions with other scenarios, thus demonstrating the wisdom of their choice. The outcome was highly successful: the community felt empowered, both with its ability to deal with technical analysis and generate ideas and visions that enable it to participate in shaping its own future. The success of the project led to a multiple of other initiatives and the creation of advocacy groups such as Partnership for Land Use Success (PLUS), an organization devoted to generating more awareness of land use issues and Scenario Analysis Group (SAG), a focus group to review and support finer-level scenario analysis with community engagement.

The participatory scenario process used in the 'Reality Check' project, represented in the diagram, can be used by any local government authority. But local authorities tend not to be benevolent. Real positive change is only ushered when a community raises its voice and concerns about its own future, and gets actively involved in shaping it.

However, community engagement in shaping futures is not limited to urban planning, or to one- or two-day visioning exercises. It can be, and in many cases ought to be, a long-term enterprise.

For the villagers of Negros Island in the Philippines, located in the Visayas, the central sweep of the archipelago, it was indeed a decade-long project. Their main livelihood came from fishing, but during the early 1990s the stocks were rapidly dwindling, and many villages were finding it hard to survive. The futurist Cesar Villanueva, who lived in the region, brought many villages together to envision a more viable future away from poverty. The villagers eagerly

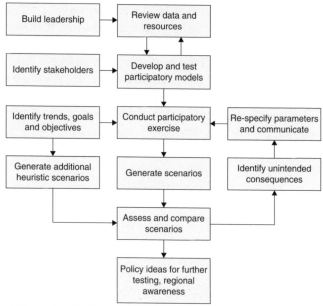

▲ The reality check process.

embraced a variety of futures methods, including visioning and backcasting, and took up futures thinking like fish to water. They created their own outreach programmes to promote futures thinking and planning. They imagined new livelihood opportunities, identified illegal fishing as the main source of their problem, and came up with ideas and projects to rehabilitate their environment. They instigated a voluntary coast-watch, and won approval from provincial authority to arrest illegal fishing boats. In collaboration with the local university they organized staff and students to help and train the fisherfolk in para-legal knowledge, leadership, gender issues, environmental care and repair and project planning, implementation, management and evaluation. Within a decade, the future they had envisioned had been realized, seen in the growth of fishing and the improvements and developments in the villages. By 2005, illegal fishing had almost ceased, with more than a hundred cases taken to court. New mangroves brought back shellfish in the estuaries. And the women began to export smocking from a community enterprise financed with microcredit managed by the villagers' network.[2]

▲ Futures studies can be applied to all kinds of problems, including fishing.

Take, as another example, the local community in Falkirk, Scotland. In 2001, the community was thrown into despair when a thousand redundancies were announced at the BP Grangemouth refinery, a major employer in the region. The redundancies were necessary, it was argued, to improve global competitiveness even though they would depress the local economy. Fortunately, a diverse group of futurists, known as the International

Futures Forum (IFF) had been established recently in nearby Fife. The group brought futurists from a number of countries

around the realization that we live in a complex world that we no longer understand or control. So long as most of our policies and actions are based on the opposite assumptions it seems many complex challenges today will remain deeply intractable. IFF was set up to explore new ways of making sense of the world that might provide the basis for more effective action and therefore a more hopeful future.[3]

In the spring of 2002, IFF brought the Falkirk community, local authorities and main employers together to produce a 'Falkirk Action Plan'. Initially the Plan consisted, as such plans normally do, of nothing more than suggestions and answers by the expert. The only thing the people of Falkirk had to do was to put the Plan into practice, 'and if it failed it would be the people's fault, not the Plan's'. The futurists pointed out that this was not the best way to operate in the complex world. A better way was to 'stretch the Plan in all directions', and be much less rigid. The community was encouraged to think in global terms, a world of open networks rather than closed clans, and to see employers such as BP not just as 'a dirty refinery and chemicals plant (which it is) but also as a creative and resourceful community (which it also is)'. Eventually, an ambitious programme of economic transformation, that involved all the actors, was developed with the title 'My Futures in Falkirk'.

It boosted the confidence of the community and led to the regeneration of the region.

The key is the involvement of 'all the actors'. Success can come only when the community is engaged fully and the entire process is open and democratic. The inclusive, open and democratic nature of futures thinking should not be seen as an ideological mandate, but as a necessary condition to solve the complex, multi-dimensional problems that we face in a globalized world. During the last decade, futurists concerned with community engagement, who tend to be 'futures activists', have produced a synthesis of futures studies and 'action learning'. Action learning is a generic term used in a variety of social and organizational settings where people learn and work together to understand and tackle the problems and issues they face. The new synthesis is called 'anticipatory action learning' and its sole purpose is to engage communities and organizations in a process of futures thinking to investigate the need for change and the nature of that change, and to chart paths towards positive and desired futures that can be realized. An effective anticipatory action learning process links individuals to social transformation, integrates different kinds and levels of appreciation of futures, creates open-ended and continually evolving conditions and contributes to intelligent action rather than formal knowledge. The process is often facilitated by a futurist, who acts as a catalyst, but the community itself engages in its own inquiry, reflection and decision-making for changing themselves and their own circumstances.

The community must identify and explore the range of alternatives it chooses to pursue.

In anticipatory action learning, the first thing to be questioned is the official future, the one that is handed down by authorities and taken for granted, so other futures can be imagined – and eventually created. Once alternative futures have been imagined, the questioning continues, and plausible desired futures are created. While the process pays attention to trends and forecasts, it is not driven by them. The overall emphasis is on mapping out future possibilities, anticipating the future using emerging issue analysis, creating alternatives using scenarios, and transforming the future through visioning, backcasting and other methods.

In anticipatory action learning workshops, the future is often mapped using a 'futures triangle'. It is simply a representation of the competing dimension of the future, emphasising the fact that the future is not fixed but is being shaped by various forces. The left-hand corner of the triangle represents the forces that are pushing the community towards a given future such as new technologies, global trends, economic opportunities, big business, migration patterns and demographic shifts. The top corner represents the forces that are pulling the community towards a specific future such as glossy advertising images of the wonderful things that the future offers, and other competing images. Finally, the right-hand corner represents the weight of the future, all those things that are holding the community back, things that cannot be changed, immovable structures and the like. The plausible futures, the ones that the community can work with, lie within the triangle.

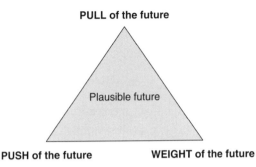

PULL of the future

Plausible future

PUSH of the future   **WEIGHT of the future**

▲ The Futures Triangle.

Anticipatory action learning workshops have frequently been used to help communities, civil servants and government organizations to anticipate future needs and shape plausible futures. For example, in Queensland, Australia, various workshops have been used to explore the contradictions that arise from the changing requirements of a society and the need for bureaucracies to respond in an agile and flexible manner – a characteristic not noted among civil servants. Various methodologies have been used in these workshops both to envision plausible futures and to shape policies which are then fed back into the bureaucratic organizations. In some workshops, futures triangles have been used to explore the influences pushing, pulling or anchoring the Public Service. In others, metaphors of the future of Queensland Public Service have been used to explore the futures of the local environment for the next 25 years, involving both members of the public and experts. Other methods used in these workshops include emerging issues analysis, used to explore what new skills will be needed in the future, what new skills are likely to emerge and examine how to build flexibility and agility in the Queensland Public Service.[4]

The best example of anticipatory action learning comes from the Shire of Maroochy, near Brisbane, in the Sunshine Coast region of South East Queensland, Australia. 'Maroochy 2025 Community Visioning Project' was initiated in January 2003 by the Maroochy Shire Council. The region faced several issues, including rapid population growth, the viability of its traditional industries, concern around sustainable development, the questions of governance and leadership and the lack of participation of the community in the decision-making process. The Council proposed a Maroochy 2025 strategy, which was presented to a meeting of key stakeholders. But the strategy was contested and it became clear that without wide-ranging involvement of the community, who preferred to sustain the unique environment, character and culture of the region, things could not move forward. The Maroochy 2025 project emerged after further wide-ranging consultations, based on the premise that neither the 'business as usual' nor 'growth mania model' were applicable but a different future had to be imagined. But what could that future be? The project did not simply aim to engage the community in an opinion-seeking exercise but to 'involve the community in activities through which they would best articulate their preferred visions for the future of their region'.[5]

These 'activities' included mapping the future with a futures triangle, visioning and backcasting, emerging issue analysis and causal layered analysis. The participants in the activities included representatives from state and local government, local academics and professionals, business representatives, community groups, schools and youth groups, local ethnic groups, indigenous communities, persons with disabilities and the general public. These participants were engaged through workshops, websites, school summits, Youth Council visioning sessions, community summits, creation of a Community Task Force, Action Planning Groups, an action planning 'Integration Night', document and literature reviews, community survey and newsletters, and articles in local newspapers. Some 3,840 people directly participated in visioning exercises, generating 3,368 community visions/ideas/goals from which the community vision statement was created. While there were inevitable clashes of ideas and worldviews, the community was open to having its assumptions challenged, and it worked effectively 'to find innovative and intuitive answers to Maroochy's future issues and problems, defining, creating, and analysing possible trends, issues, and scenarios for Maroochy Shire'. Its vision and solutions became part of the Maroochy Shire Council's 2005–2009 Corporate Plan, and were implemented successfully. It is now considered as one of the 'best practice case studies' in anticipatory action learning literature.

There is considerable evidence to suggest that futures thinking can empower a community, motivate it to imagine better futures and work towards pragmatic solutions. Beyond all the abstract ideas and theories, futures thought and action is all about taking the future into your own hand. Futures studies can be used by any community, anywhere, determined to shape a more viable and sustainable future for itself.

What's next?

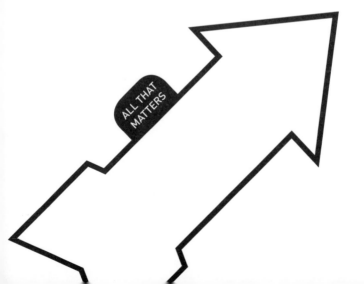

ALL THAT MATTERS

'What comes next?', the respected magazine *Scientific American* asked a collection of 'visionary scientists'. The answers, which appeared in a special issue of the magazine called 'The End', consisted of typical trend projections.[1] Synthetic biology will enable us to design life to order, there will be tailor-made medicine, the riddle of consciousness will be solved, and we will have infinite 'storage capacity were among them. Of course, some of these predictions may come true; some may not.

However, our record for predictions, particularly those of 'the scientists', is not very impressive. How we predicted the much heralded year 2000, for example, changed regularly during the span of the twentieth century. At the 1900 Paris Exhibition, the world's leading scientist thought that we could not travel more than 250 miles an hour, or launch rockets into space, or anyone would bother to buy radios or light bulbs. In 1950, *Popular Mechanics* predicted chemistry would revolutionize our homes: plates would be dissolved instead of washed, all our furniture would consist of washable synthetics so they could be hosed down, and used rayon underpants would be converted to sweets for children.[2] A decade later, predictions of manned trips to Mars were as common as reality shows. In the mid-1970s, NASA was predicting space colonies by 2000. And so it went on as we approached the year 2000 when, it was predicted, we would face a computing meltdown thanks to the Y2K bug.[3]

Fascinating though they are, predictions are largely a side issue. The future is less and less a domain of prediction, and more and more an arena of change and action. It is also a territory where we seek meaning for our existence, while our very existence as a human civilization comes under question. American futurist Bruce Tonn has argued that western culture, institutions and policymaking techniques and processes are inherently biased against the future and constitute the strongest hazard to shaping a viable future for humanity; thus they threaten the very existence of 'intelligent life' on the planet. Take culture, for example. 'Most cognitive effort is directed toward production and consumption', writes Tonn. 'During every waking hour of every day of every year', most of our thoughts 'are directed toward making money or engaging in some aspect related to consumption' such as entertainment, watching television, or shopping. In contrast, 'time and thought devoted to sustainability issues is less than minimal. As a culture, very little consideration is given to long-term issues.' Most of our institutions are designed to promote the short-term goals of production and consumption.

The mantra for the private sector is 'shareholder satisfaction today!' Firms must make a profit, preferably every quarter of every year. If they fail to do so for more than a few quarters, they will cease to exist. The advent of information technology and globalization of the world's economy has resulted in a panic of change and competition. The rush to produce and sell and make money and count the results is ubiquitous. Given a perspective of several millions of years, this rush, which is jeopardizing long-term sustainability, is misguided. As an institution, the private sector has few incentives to think long-term.[4]

Our political systems too are designed to ignore 'future-oriented considerations that necessarily involve unknowable future generations and much uncertainty in the decision making process'. Policy and decision analysts work hard to keep the system of production and consumption going.

A future you deserve

Live more.

Connect more.

Smile more.

Fake more.

Find more.

Consume more.

Discover more.

Share more.

Learn more.

Make more.

Play more.

Think yourself ...

No more. No more ... no more ... no more.

THE FUTURE IS BROKEN

Advertisement for UK Channel 4's dramas exploring the future, 'Black Mirror'.

Futures thinking becomes meaningful when it identifies and critiques potential hazards that could close the future or colonize it, and attempts to make sense of the present. In all futures work, whatever the tradition, wherever it is undertaken (whether in universities, research institutions, corporations, government institutions or communities), whoever is involved (academics, researchers, consultants or activists), there is one overriding concern: how to make the future more real, more accessible, more immediate and hence make the present the domain where action is taken to transform the coming decades.

The future may be located on some distant horizon, but it is also right here, with us. What we do today as individuals and communities, corporations and nation states has direct implications for the future we will inherit. Things change but the future is the only arena where we can actively change things for the better and that change has to start from where we are today.

As such, futures thinking is only partly about what might happen in the future. Mostly it is about what we would like to happen, and how we can make it happen – what we could do to shape positive and viable futures for all humanity. Futures studies pursue this goal by challenging the conventional images of the future, by inspiring imaginative leaps, by envisioning other potentials and possibilities, and by making human agency the centre of future-oriented action. There are no right or wrong answers in exploring the future. But the journey itself expands and enhances your capabilities of understanding and handling future issues. And, in the process, you may actually realize the future you desire.

After examining various dimensions of 'the future', taking a short tour of its history, looking at numerous methods used for studying and exploring the future, and examining how these methods have been used to empower communities and organizations, there is only one thing we can say with certainty: there are many alternatives, many ways to open and close the future, and many different directions for travelling towards the future. Futures studies try to ensure that all the viable options remain open and pregnant with potentials.

The American actor and comedian W.C. Field was once asked: 'what do you think about the future?' 'Why should I think of the future?', he shot back. 'What has the future done for me?' Futures studies invite you to do something about the future so that the future may do something for you and you leave something for future generations that enables them to survive and thrive. The future is not just an imaginary distance over the horizon, it is the domain of your existence. If you are alive today, you could be alive 30, 40, 50 years from now.

And if you are alive, the diversity of alternative futures, pushing and pulling you in various directions, need to know: what are you doing tomorrow?

5 indispensable resources

1. Wendell Bell's *The Foundations of Futures Studies* (New Brunswick: Transaction Publishers, 1997, two volumes) is an obligatory text for anyone with a serious interest in futures studies. It provides a succinct introduction to the history of the field, explores assumptions and epistemology of futures studies, dips into various methods, and provides some practical strategies for judging preferable futures – all within a humanistic framework.

2. *The Knowledge Base of Futures Studies* (ed. Richard Slaughter, Indooroopilly, Queensland: Foresight International, 2005), is a veritable mine of information on (almost) everything to do with futures studies. Most of the contributors to the three volumes are noted futurists who have made original contributions to the field. The 'Pro' CD version includes two additional volumes, one devoted to biographical accounts and the other on 'synergies, case studies and implementation'.

3. *State of the Future* annual reports by the Millennium Project (Washington D.C.) contain the latest ideas and thoughts of experts on global issues, futures of emerging technologies, as well as issues of ethics, education and sustainability. Each report contains a string of new futures scenarios, survey of futures studies around the world and examinations of futures methodologies. The reports come out both as a condensed printed version and a massive CD.

4. Futures Studies Bookshelf, a resource developed by the World Futures Studies Federation, contains bibliographies of books relating to the future and futures studies. It covers English, Swedish, Spanish, Portuguese, Hebrew, Hungarian and Farsi languages, with books listed in decades, starting with 'pre-1950 and classics'

http://www.wfsf.org/index.php?option=com_content&view=category&id=100&Itemid=125.

5. Forwiki is a platform for the development of a futures studies and foresight wiki (http://www.forwiki.ro/wiki/Main_Page). It is edited, modified and constantly updated by professional futurists and academics.

10 refereed journals

6. *Futures*, the monthly journal of policy, planning and futures studies, is the oldest and most established primary journal in the field. Rigorously refereed, it is a multidisciplinary journal concerned with medium- and long-term futures of cultures and civilizations, science and technology, economics and politics, environment and the planet and individual and communities.

7. *Foresight*, a bi-monthly journal concerned with the study of the futures, focuses on social, political and economic science, sustainable development, horizon scanning, management of uncertainty, complexity and risk, methods, tools and techniques, and scientific and technological change and its implications for society and policy.

8. *Technological Forecasting and Social Change* focuses, as the name suggests, on technological forecasting and examines the future in relation to environmental and technological factors.

9. *Journal of Futures Studies*, published quarterly by Tamkang University Press, explores issues of epistemology, methods and applied and alternative futures.

10. *World Future Review*, started as *Futures Research Quarterly*, a professional journal published by the World Future Society, Washington D.C., but merged with the *Futures Survey*, also published by WFS, in 2013. It describes itself as 'a journal of strategic foresight', 'the top forum for all who are professionally involved in exploring trends and alternatives for society'.

11. *Futuribles International*, founded in 1975 by Hugues de Jouvenel, is a multidisciplinary journal that comes out twice a year. In French, with abstracts in English.

12. *World Futures*, published eight times a year, is a journal of global education with some futures studies content.

13. *Time and Society*, an international peer-reviewed journal, explores time-related changes across disciplines and organizations, and occasionally looks at future time.

14. *The Journal of Forecasting* is an international journal concerned with theoretical, computational and methodological issues, with focus on business, government, technology and the environment.

15. *Policy Futures in Education* focuses on innovative futures-oriented thinking in education theory and policy from diverse viewpoints.

5 magazines

16. *The Futurist*, the bi-monthly magazine of World Future Society, Washington D.C., is one of the oldest and most established magazines in the futures field. It explores the technological, scientific, environmental, social and policy trends shaping our collective future.

17. *Manoa Journal for Fried and Half Fried Ideas (about the future)* is an online 'drive thru' magazine of futures

ideas and issues, and occasional papers: http://www.friedjournal.com/.

18. *Wired*, the monthly print publication of culture, opinion and technology, often covers futures-related topics and issues.

19. *The Club of Amsterdam Journal* is a free online magazine devoted to 'shaping your future in the knowledge society', published every two weeks, that you can receive by email.

20. *EcoMag*, available on the EcoLab website (http://www.ecolab.com), is a magazine about art, design and sustainability that explores issues at the root of the ecological crisis.

10 main organizations

21. World Futures Studies Federation, which brings together futures professionals and activists, as well as organizations and institutions, is one of the oldest and most established futures organizations. Its conferences are particularly noted for their diversity and dynamism.

22. World Future Society is an organization of people dedicated to the future, based in Washington D.C. It publishes the *Futurist* magazine and holds exceptionally well-attended conferences.

23. The Millennium Project, a global futures institution, works to develop concrete action plans to achieve the Millennium Development Goals and to reverse the grinding poverty, hunger and disease affecting the world's poor. The Project was commissioned by the United Nations Secretary-General in 2002, and has now become a wide-ranging international network of futurists consisting of 'nodes' in almost every country. It produces the impressive annual *State of the Future* reports, and offers a dynamic, live Delphi on a wide range of issues. It is an invaluable source of information, tools, methodologies and other resources on the future.

24. The Club of Rome is one of the oldest and most influential global networks of eminent individuals. Established in 1968, it is responsible for a string of ground-breaking reports, such as *The Limits to Growth* and *Mankind at the Turning Point*.

25. The World Future Council is a council of 50 eminent individuals interested in bringing the interests of future generations to the centre of policymaking. The Council aims to 'identify the most crucial problems which will determine the future of humanity through integrated and forward-looking analysis; to evaluate alternative scenarios for the future and to assess risks, choices and opportunities; to develop and propose practical solutions to the challenges identified; [and] to communicate the new insights and knowledge derived from this analysis to decision-makers in the public and private sectors'.

26. The Foresight Network is a professional body of futurists and foresight experts that promotes shared knowledge, opportunities, experiences and guidance among its members.

27. The Tomorrow Network is a British network of individuals interested in futures work. It holds three or four Network events a year with distinguished speakers where futures issues are debated and discussed. Membership is free. http://www.tomorrowproject.net/index.shtml?page=network.

28. Institute for Alternative Futures, a non-profit organization founded in 1977, is a leader in the creation of preferred futures. Based in Alexandria, Virginia, it focuses on sustainability, health, education and issues of governance.

29. Lifeboat Foundation is a non-profit non-governmental organization dedicated to helping humanity survive

existential risks of increasingly powerful technologies, such as genetic engineering, nanotechnology, robotics and artificial intelligence. It was established with the help of the world's first bitcoin endowment fund.

30. Centre for Futures Studies is an Egyptian think tank and network of futurists based in Cairo. It undertakes research in such areas as sustainability of Egyptian cities, food security and visions of Egypt, and offers training courses in futures studies. http://www.future.idsc.gov.eg/FutureWWW/start/index.jsp.

12 important academic institutions

31. The Hawaii Research Center for Futures Studies (*Hawaii Futures*), established by the Hawaii State Legislature in 1971, is one of the world's most renowned institutions for futures research, consulting and education. Located within the Department of Political Science, College of Social Sciences at the University of Hawaii at Manoa, it has been instrumental in the education of four decades of futurists, in the development and spread of judicial and educational foresight and in bringing foresight and futures thinking to organizations, agencies and businesses around the world.

32. Futures Program at University of Houston, Texas, the other main institution in the US responsible for producing a generation of futurists. It offers education and training in futures thinking and methodologies in a variety of formats.

33. Institute of Futures Studies is an independent, interdisciplinary research centre for advanced social research that promotes future-oriented perspectives in Swedish research. Based in Stockholm, it is renowned for its pioneering research during the 1970s and 1980s, and the World Values Survey.

34. The Laboratory for Investigation in Prospective and Strategy at Conservatoire des Arts et Metiers, Paris, is a world leader in scenario planning, strategic management, future trends and uncertainties, foresight methods and futures studies. It also offers graduate courses in applied futures studies, evaluation and futures research on technology.

35. The Faculty of Business and Enterprise, Swinburne University of Technology, now incorporates the famous Australian Foresight Institute, which was a hotbed of futures studies during the 1990s. It is now the home of 'Integral Futures', and has a dynamic futures studies programme.

36. University of Sunshine Coast, Australia, is the home of Anticipatory Action Learning. Its Faculty of Arts and Social Sciences offers a number of masters and doctorate programmes in futures studies.

37. The Corvinus University of Budapest has produced a generation of East European futurists. It has active and much sought-after undergraduate and postgraduate programmes.

38. Finland Futures Academy, a university network, is one of the leading futures studies institutions in the world. It offers a 'Futures Studies Subsidiary Program' in different universities throughout Finland.

39. The Center for Futures Studies at Tamkang University, Taiwan, has been teaching futures studies at undergraduate and postgraduate level for decades. The Graduate Institute of Futures Studies, in conjunction with the School of Education, also offers a Master's of Education with an emphasis on Futures Studies. The university publishes *The Journal of Futures Studies*.

40. Universidad Externo de Colombia, Bogota, leads futures studies in Latin America. Its courses emphasize both theory and practice of futures studies.

41. Department of Futures Studies, University of Kerala, is a major centre of futures research and education in India. Established in 1990/91 by a government decree, the department pursues research in technology management and forecasting, system dynamics, and modelling and simulation, and offers masters and PhD courses in futures studies with emphasis on technology management.

42. Future of Humanity Institute, Oxford University, a multidisciplinary research institute, brings scholars together from a range of disciplines to examine big-picture questions about humanity and its prospects.

20 websites

There are numerous websites exploring the future from various perspectives. Here are some I have found useful.

43. Global Simulation Workshop. Run the world with this interactive and innovative game designed to create awareness of global issues.
http://www.worldgame.org/.

44. FutureScanner. Vote for your favourite predictions.
http://www.memebox.com/futurescanner.

45. Resilient Futures. Learn to cope with complex change by joining other decision-makers and innovators in a 'next practice' strategic framework.
http://www.memebox.com/futurescanner

46. Forward Engagement. Work on turning complex, interactive and longer-range issues into public policy.
http://www.forwardengagement.org/.

47. Forward Looks. Join Europe's scientific community to develop medium- to long-term views and analyses of future research developments and define research agendas at national and European level.
http://www.esf.org/index.php?id=54.

48. Futures Scenarios. Explore the interaction between climate change and peak oil using scenario planning.
http://www.futurescenarios.org/.

49. The European Foresight Monitoring Network. Join other experts in a Foresight Knowledge Sharing Platform.
http://ec.europa.eu/research/foresight/.

50. The Long Now Foundation. Move from 'faster/cheaper' mindset to 'slower/better' thinking within a framework of the next thousand years.
http://longnow.org/.

51. Acceleration Studies Foundation. Explore our increasingly accelerating technological and computational world through roadmapping, forecasting, scenarios and other data-driven research.
http://www.accelerating.org/futuresalon.html.

52. World Shift Network. Focus on much-neglected human abilities of self-awareness, compassion and wisdom.
http://www.worldshiftnetwork.org/home/index.html.

53. RAND Corporation. Explore issues of security at the original think tank (with emphasis firmly on the tank) and download lots of reports and publications.
http://www.rand.org/.

54. Shaping Tomorrow. Join in shaping the world of the future and make better decisions today.
http://www.shapingtomorrow.com/.

55. Global Scenario Group. Join an international initiative to explore alternative futures.
http://gsg.org/.

56. Foresight International. An invaluable site from Richard Slaughter, futurist and foresight expert, with papers, videos, blogs and a string of e-books to download.
http://www.foresightinternational.com.au/.

57. Infinite Futures. Join futurist Wendy Schultz on her site and be rewarded with a bundle of essays, resources, tools and toys. http://www.infinitefutures.com/.

58. Global Foresight Network. Design better futures with a network of researchers, thinkers and consultants working on strategic foresight. http://www.globalforesight.net/.

59. Metafutures. Join the husband and wife team of Sohail Inayatullah and Ivana Milojevic to explore future-oriented issues with a focus on the work of futurists from Australia and New Zealand. http://www.metafuture.org/.

60. Hawaii Futures. Learn how futures philosophy is being used to shape Hawaiian urbanism within a 'forward-thinking, 100-year framework for urban redevelopment and ecosystem restoration'. http://www.hawaii-futures.com/.

61. Alternative Futures. See how another future is being created in India through meaningful policy, social and technological alternatives and innovations for development and social change. http://www.alternativefutures.org.in/.

62. WFSF Iberoamerica. The Latin American arm of the World Futures Studies Federation, it contains essays, analysis, links to numerous other Spanish sites and a lively magazine http://www.wfsf-iberoamerica.org/.

8 documentary films

63. 'What if?' is a series of half-hour documentaries from the BBC World Service exploring visions of the future. It asks such questions as: what if women ruled the world? What if everyone had a car? What if you could mine the moon? The answers are mostly technological solutions. http://www.bbc.co.uk/news/world-21069026.

64. 'The Cleantech Future' asks the question that BBC does not: what if we could live in a clean world? It charts the visible signs of a new future from China, Thailand, Europe to the US looking at green mobility powered by sustainable energy, dyeing textiles using recycled CO2 and the production of clean drinking water using nanotechnology. http://topdocumentaryfilms.com/cleantech-future/.

65. '2057: City of the Future' looks at the metropolis 50 years from now.
http://topdocumentaryfilms.com/2057-the-city-of-the-future/.

66. 'Future Life on Earth' is a high-tech look at how life will evolve and how technology will use our natural resources.
http://topdocumentaryfilms.com/future-life-on-earth/.

67. 'The Future of Food' is a fascinating investigation into genetically modified food; it examines the complex web of market and political forces that are changing what we eat as huge multinational corporations seek to control the world's food system.
http://topdocumentaryfilms.com/the-future-of-food/.

68. 'Future is Wild' looks at who or what would survive after the earth has been affected by massive climatic and geological changes.
http://topdocumentaryfilms.com/future-is-wild/.

69. 'Earth 2100: The Final Century of Civilisation': could we be reaching the end of civilization as we know it? Discuss.
http://topdocumentaryfilms.com/earth-2100-final-century-of-civilization/.

70. 'Beyond Human': prepare for machines that are more human than humans.
http://topdocumentaryfilms.com/beyond-human/.

30 key texts (in chronological order)

71. Gordon, T.J. and Helmer, O., *Report on a Long-Range Forecasting Study* (Santa Monica: RAND, 1964).

72. Flechtheim, Ossip, *History and Futurology* (Meisenheim am Glan: Anton Hian, 1966).

73. Kahn, Herman and Wiener, Anthony J., *The Year 2000: A Framework for Speculation on the Next Thirty-Three Years* (New York: Macmillan, 1967).

74. Jantsch, Erich, *Technological Forecasting in Perspective* (Paris: OECD,1967).

75. de Jouvenel, Bertrand, *The Art of Conjecture* (New York: Basic Books, 1967).

76. Jungk, Robert and Galtung, John (eds), *Mankind 2000* (London: Allen and Unwin, 1969).

77. Meadows, Donella *et al.*, *The Limits to Growth* (New York: Universe,1972).

78. Bell, Daniel, *The Coming of Post-Industrial Society: A Venture in Social Forecasting* (New York: Basic Books, 1973).

79. Polak, Fred, *The Image of the Future* (Amsterdam: Elsevier,1973).

80. Kothari, Rajni, *Footsteps into the Future* (Delhi: Longman, 1974).

81. Ciba Foundation, *The Future as an Academic Discipline* (Amsterdam: Elsevier,1975).

82. Godet, Michael, 'Introduction to la prospective: Seven key ideas and one scenario method', Futures 2 (2), 134–157, March 1976; and *Creating Futures: Scenario Planning as a Strategic Tool* (Paris: Economica, 2001).

83. Herrera, Amilcar (ed.), *Catastrophe or New Society? A Latin American World Model* (Ottawa: International Development Centre, 1976).

84. Cornish, Edward (ed.), *The Study of the Future* (Bethesda: World Future Society, 1977).

85. Freeman, Christopher and Johada, Marie (eds), *World Futures: The Great Debate* (London: Martin Robertson, 1978).

86. Waddington, C.H., *The Man-Made Future* (London: Croom Helm, 1978).

87. Clark, I.F., *The Pattern of Expectation: 1644–2001* (London: Jonathan Cape, 1979).

88. Masini, Eleonora Barbieri (ed.), *Visions of Desirable Societies* (Oxford: Pergamon, 1983); *Why Futures Studies?* (London: Grey Seal, 1993); and Masini, Eleonora and Sasson, Albert (eds), *The Futures of Cultures* (Paris: UNESCO, 1994).

89. Brundtland, Gro Harlem, *Our Common Future* (Oxford: Oxford University Press, 1987).

90. Nandy, Ashis, 'Shaman, savages and the wilderness: on the audibility of dissent and the future of civilisations', *Alternatives*, XIV (3), July 1989; and *Traditions, Tyranny and Utopias* (Delhi: Oxford University Press, 1992).

91. Tough, Allen, *Crucial Questions About the Future* (Lanham, MD: University Press of America, 1991).

92. Sardar, Ziauddin, 'Colonising the Future: The "Other" Dimension of Future Studies', *Futures*, 25 (3), 1993; Sardar, Ziauddin (ed.), *Rescuing All Our Futures: The Future of Futures Studies* (London: Admantine, 1996); and Sardar, Ziauddin, 'Welcome to postnormal times', *Futures*, 42 (5), 435–44, June 2010.

100 Ideas

93. Inayatullah, Sohail, 'From "who am I?" to "when am I?": framing the shape and time of the future', *Futures*, 25 (3), 235–53, April 1993; and Wildman, Paul and Inayatullah, Sohail, 'Ways of knowing, civilization, communication and the pedagogies of the future', *Futures*, 28 (8), 723–40, October 1996.

94. Ogutu, Gilbert, Malaska, Penitti and Kojola, Johanna (eds), *Futures Beyond Poverty - Ways and Means Out of the Current Stalemate* (Turku, Finland: Finland Futures Research Centre, 1995).

95. Slaughter, Richard, *The Foresight Principle* (London: Adamantine,1995).

96. Henderson, Hazel, *Building a Win-Win World: Life beyond Global Economic Warfare* (San Francisco: Berrett-Koehler Publishers, 1996).

97. Batty, Michael and Cole, Sam, 'Time and Space: Geographic Perspective on the Future', Special Issue *Futures*, 29 (4–5), May–June 1997.

98. Dator, James A. and Kim, Tae-Chang (eds), *Co-Creating Public Philosophies for Future Generations* (London: Adamantine Press, 1998).

99. Adesida, Olugbenga and Oteh, Arunma (eds) *Visions of the Future of Africa* (Twickenham: Adamantine Press Ltd, 1999).

100. Gary, Jay E., 'The future according to Jesus: a Galilean model of foresight', *Futures*, 40 (7), 630–42, September 2008.

Bibliography

Abdalla, Ismail-Sabri *et al.*, *Images of the Arab Future* (London: Frances Pinter, 1983).

Al-Farabi, *On the Perfect State*, trans by Richard Walzar, Great Books of the Islamic World (Cambridge: Kazi Publications, 1997).

Andersson, Jenny, 'The great future debate and the struggle for the world', *American Historical Review Forum*, 1411–30, December 2012.

Berry, B.J.L., 'Long Waves and Geography', *Futures*, 29 (4–5), 301–10, May–June 1997.

Bell, Wendell, *Foundations of Futures Studies* (New Brunswick: Transaction Publishers, 1997), two volumes.

Bloch, Ernst, *The Principle of Hope* (Cambridge, MA: MIT Press, 1995).

Boulding, Elise, 'Women's visions of the future', in Masini, Eleonora (ed.), *Visions of desirable societies* (London: Pergamon, 1983).

Chakraborty, Arnab, 'Enhancing the role of participatory scenario planning processes: lessons from Reality Check exercises', *Futures*, 43 (4), 387–99, May 2011.

Cole, Sam, 'Global issues and futures: a theory and pedagogy for heuristic modelling', *Futures*, 40 (9), 777–87, 2008.

Collie, Natalie, 'Cities of the imagination: science fiction, urban space, and community engagement in urban planning', *Futures*, 43 (4), 424–31, May 2011.

Dator, Jim, 'The WFSF and Me', *Futures*, 37 (5), 371–85, June 2005.

Dator, Jim, 'The future lies behind: thirty years of teaching futures studies', *American Behavioral Scientist*, 42 (3), 298–319, 1998.

Dortmans, Peter J., 'Forecasting, backcasting, migration landscapes and strategic planning maps', *Futures*, 37 (4), 273–85, May 2005.

Dreborg, K.H., 'Essence of backcasting', *Futures*, 28 (9), 813–28, 1996.

van der Duin, Patrick, *Knowing Tomorrow? How Science Deals With the Future* (Delft: Eburon, 2007).

Flechtheim, Ossip K., *History and Futurology* (Meisenheim am Glan: Verlag Anton Hain, 1966).

Godet, Michel, *Creating Futures: Scenario Planning as a Strategic Management Tool* (Paris: Economica, 2001).

Gould, Steve, 'Maroochy 2025 Community Visioning & Action - A Case Study of Anticipatory Action Learning Practices in Use Within

Maroochy Shire, Queensland, Australia', *Journal of Futures Studies*, 10(1), 125–32, August 2005.

van der Helm, Ruud, 'The vision phenomenon: towards a theoretical underpinning of visions of the future and the process of envisioning', *Futures*, 41 (2) 96–104, March 2009.

Helmer, Olaf, 'Science', *Science Journal*, 3 (10), 49–51, October 1967.

Henderson, Hazel, *Building a win–win world: Life beyond global economic warfare* (San Francisco: Berret-Koehler, 1996).

Herrera, A.O. et al., *Catastrophe or New Society? A Latin American World Model* (Ottawa: DRC, 1976).

Hiltunen, Elina, 'Was it a wild card or just our blindness to gradual change?', *Journal of Futures Studies*, 11 (2), 61–74, November 2006.

Inayatullah, Sohail, 'From "who am I" to "when am I?"', *Futures*, 25 (3), 235–53, April 1993.

Inayatullah, Sohail, 'Six pillars: futures thinking for transforming', *Foresight*, 10 (1), 4–21, 2008.

Inayatullah, Sohail, *Questioning the Future* (Taipei: Tamkang University, 2002).

Joshi, Nandini, 'Women can change the future', *Futures*, 24 (9) 931–7, November 1992.

de Jouvenel, Bertrand, *The Art of Conjecture* (New York: Basic Books, 1967).

Jungk, Robert, *Tomorrow is Already Here* (London: Hart-Davis, 1954).

Jungk, Robert and Galtung, J. (eds), *Mankind 2000* (London: Allen and Unwin, 1969).

Kahn, Herman and Wiener, Anthony J., *The Year 2000: A Framework for Speculation on the Next Thirty-Three Years* (New York: Macmillan, 1967).

Kahn, Herman, *The Emerging Japanese Superstate* (London: Andre Deutsch, 1971).

Kennedy, Paul, *The Rise and Fall of the Great Powers* (New York: Random House, 1989).

Khaldun, Ibn, *The Muqaddimah: An Introduction to History* (London: Routledge and Kegan Paul, 1967), original written circa 1380.

Kothari, Rajni, *The Footsteps into the Future* (Delhi: Orient Longman, 1974).

Kumar, Krishan, *Utopianism* (Buckingham: Open University Press, 1991).

Leicester, Graham, 'Sustaining human aspirations: action learning in Falkirk', *Journal of Futures Studies*, 10 (1), 123–4, August 2005.

Mahfouz, Naguib, *The Journey of Ibn Fattouma* (New York: Anchor Books, 1993).

Masini, Eleonora Barbieri, *Why Futures Studies* (London: Grey Seal, 1993).

May, Graham, *The Future is Ours* (London: Adamantine, 1996).

Mesarovic, M. and Pestel, E., *Mankind at the Turning Point* (London: Hutchinson,1974).

Meadows, Donella *et al.*, *The Limits to Growth* (New York: Universe,1972).

Nandy, Ashis, *Traditions, Tyranny and Utopias* (Delhi: Oxford University Press, 1987).

Piganiol, Pierre, 'Introduction: futurology and prospective study', *International Social Science Journal*, 21 (4), 515–26, 1969.

Polak, Frederik, *The Image of the Future* (Amsterdam: Elsevier, 1973; original Dutch edition 1968).

Rossel, Pierre, Miller, Riel and Jorgensen, Ulrik (eds), 'Weak Signals', Special issue *Futures*, 44 (2), 195–276, April 2012.

Sardar, Ziauddin, *The Future of Muslim Civilization* (London: Croom Helm, 1979; second edition London: Mansell, 1985).

Sardar, Ziauddin, *Islamic Futures: The Shape of Ideas to Come* (London: Mansell,1985).

Sardar, Ziauddin, *Orientalism* (Buckingham: Open University Press, 1999).

Sardar, Ziauddin (ed.), 'The Morning After', Special issue *Futures*, 32 (1), January–February 2000.

Sardar, Ziauddin and Cubitt, Sean (eds), *Aliens R US: The Other in Science Fiction Cinema* (London: Pluto, 2002).

Sardar, Ziauddin, 'The Namesake: Futures, futures studies, futurology, futuristic, foresight – What's in a name?', *Futures*, 42 (3), 177–84, April 2010.

Slaughter, Richard, 'Futures Concept', in Slaughter, Richard, *The Knowledge Base of Futures Studies* (Hawthorn: DDM Media Group, 1996).

Slaughter, Richard A., 'What difference does "integral" make?', *Futures*, 40 (2), 120–37, March 2008.

van Steenbergen, Bart, 'The First Fifteen Years: a Personal View of the Early History of the WFSF (1967–1982)', *Futures*, 37 (5), 355–60, 2005.

Stevenson, Tony, 'Courage and resilience: creating Filipino futures', *Futures*, 39 (4), 463–74, May 2007.

Strauss, William and Howe, Neil, *Generations: The History of America's Future* (New York: William Morrow, 1991).

Suvin, Darko, 'On the poetics of the science fiction genre', in Rose, Mark (ed.), *Science Fiction: Twentieth Century Views* (New York: Prentice Hall, 1972).

Teske, Kate, 'Futures in government: use of anticipatory action learning to explore public service futures', *Journal of Futures Studies*, 10 (1), 119–22, August 2005.

Toffler, Alvin, *Future Shock* (New York: Random House, 1970).

Tonn, Bruce E., 'Ensuring the future', Special issue, *Futures* 32 (1), 17–26, January–February 2000.

Tough, Allen, *Crucial Questions About the Future* (New York: University Press of America, 1991).

Toynbee, Arnold, *A Study of History* (Oxford: Oxford University Press, 1934).

Tufayl, Ibn, 'The Story of Hayy ibn Yaqzān (1169–79)', in *Two Andalusian Philosophers*, trans by Jim Colville (London: Kegan Paul International, 1999).

UNDP, *Reclaiming the Future: A Manual for Futures Studies for African Planners* (London: Tycooly International, 1986).

Voros, Joseph, 'Integral futures: an approach to futures inquiry', *Futures*, 40 (2), 190–201, March 2008.

Wells, H.G., 'Wanted; Professors of Foresight', BBC Radio Broadcast, 19 November 1932.

Wells, H.G., *When the Sleeper Wakes* (London: Penguin classics, 2005).

Wright, David, 'Alternative futures: Aml scenarios and Minority Report', *Futures*, 40 (5), 473–88, June 2008.

Wright, George and Cairns, George, *Scenario Thinking: Practical Approaches to the Future* (London: Palgrave Macmillan, 2011).

Notes

Chapter 1

1. Tough, Allen, *Crucial Questions About the Future* (New York: University Press of America, 1991), p. 1.
2. *Hemisphere*, April 2012, pp. 78–84; hemispheremagazine.com.
3. Wright, David, 'Alternative futures: AmI scenarios and Minority Report', *Futures*, 40 (5) 473–88, June 2008.
4. World Futures Studies Federation website: http://www.wfsf.org/index.php?option=com_content&view=article&id=74&Itemid=135.
5. Fleetwood Mac, 'Rumours', album, Warner Brothers, 1977.

Chapter 2

1. Khaldun, Ibn, *The Muqaddimah: An Introduction to History* (London: Routledge and Kegan Paul, 1967), original written circa 1380.
2. Toynbee, Arnold, *A Study of History* (Oxford: Oxford University Press, 1934).
3. Kennedy, Paul, *The Rise and Fall of the Great Powers* (New York: Random House, 1989).
4. Berry, B.J.L., 'Long Waves and Geography', *Futures*, 29 (4–5), 301–10, May–June 1997.
5. On 'wild cards', see Hiltunen, Elina, 'Was it a wild card or just our blindness to gradual change?', *Journal of Futures Studies*, 11 (2), 61–74, November 2006.
6. Slaughter and others suggest that the 'extended present' stretches 100 years back to our grandparents and 100 years forward to our grandchildren. I disagree!

Chapter 3

1. Helmer, Olaf, 'Science', *Science Journal*, 3 (10), 49–51, October 1967; quoted by Jenny Andersson in her excellent paper, 'The great future debate and the struggle for the world', *American Historical Review Forum*, 1411–30, December 2012. See also Connelly, Matthew *et al.*, 'General, I have fought just as many nuclear wars as you have: forecasts, future scenarios, and the politics of Armageddon', and Engerman, David C., 'Introduction: histories of the future and the futures of history', both in the same issue of AHR Forum; and Gordon, T.J. and Helmer, Olaf, *Report on a Long-Range Forecasting Study* (Santa Monica: RAND, 1964).
2. Kahn, Herman and Wiener, Anthony J., *The Year 2000: A Framework for Speculation on the Next Thirty-Three Years* (New York: Macmillan, 1967).

3. Kahn, Herman, *The Emerging Japanese Superstate* (London: Andre Deutsch, 1971).
4. Flechtheim, Ossip K., *History and Futurology* (Meisenheim am Glan: Verlag Anton Hain, 1966).
5. Polak, Frederik, *The Image of the Future* (Amsterdam: Elsevier,1973); original Dutch edition, 1968.
6. Jungk, Robert, *Tomorrow is Already Here* (London: Hart-Davis, 1954).
7. de Jouvenel, Bertrand, *The Art of Conjecture* (New York: Basic Books, 1967).
8. Meadows, Donella *et al.*, *The Limits to Growth* (New York: Universe,1972).
9. Toffler, Alvin, *Future Shock* (New York: Random House, 1970).
10. Piganiol, Pierre, 'Introduction: futurology and prospective study', *International Social Science Journal*, 21 (4), 515–26, 1969.
11. Jungk, R. and Galtung, J. (eds), *Mankind 2000* (London: Allen and Unwin, 1969), p. 10.
12. Dator, Jim, 'The WFSF and Me', *Futures*, 37 (5), 371–85, June 2005.
13. van Steenbergen, Bart, 'The First Fifteen Years: a Personal View of the Early History of the WFSF (1967–1982)', *Futures*, 37 (5), 355–60, 2005.
14. Dator, Jim, 'The WFSF and Me', *op cit.*
15. Kothari, Rajni, *The Footsteps into the Future* (Delhi: Orient Longman, 1974).
16. Abdalla, Ismail-Sabri *et al.*, *Images of the Arab Future* (London: Frances Pinter, 1983).
17. Mesarovic, M. and Pestel, E., *Mankind at the Turning Point* (London: Hutchinson, 1974).
18. Sardar, Ziauddin, *The Future of Muslim Civilization* (London: Croom Helm, 1979; second edition London: Mansell, 1985).
19. Herrera, A.O. *et al.*, *Catastrophe or New Society? A Latin American World Model* (Ottawa: DRC, 1976).
20. UNDP, *Reclaiming the Future: A Manual for Futures Studies for African Planners* (London: Tycooly International, 1986), p. 1.

Chapter 4

1. Wells, H.G., 'Wanted; Professors of Foresight', BBC Radio Broadcast, 19 November, 1932.
2. Bell, Wendell, *Foundations of Futures Studies* (New Brunswick: Transaction Publishers, 1997), volume 1, Chapter 3, pp. 140–57 .
3. *Ibid.*, pp. 144–5.
4. Masini, Eleonora Barbieri, *Why Futures Studies* (London: Grey Seal, 1993), pp. 6–10.

5. Dator, Jim, 'The future lies behind: thirty years of teaching futures studies', *American Behavioral Scientist*, 42 (3), 298–319, 1998.
6. Sardar, Ziauddin, 'The Namesake: Futures, futures studies, futurology, futuristic, foresight – What's in a name?', *Futures*, 42 (3), 177–84, April 2010.
7. Slaughter, Richard, 'Futures Concept' in Slaughter, Richard, *The Knowledge Base of Futures Studies* (Hawthorn: DDM Media Group, 1996), volume 1, pp. 93–4.
8. Inayatullah, Sohail, 'From "who am I" to "when am I?"', *Futures*, 25 (3), 235–53, April 1993.
9. Inayatullah, Sohail, 'Six pillars: futures thinking for transforming', *Foresight*, 10 (1), 4–21, 2008.
10. http://wfsf.merlot.org/studies/.

Chapter 5
1. See Strauss, William and Howe, Neil, *Generations*: *The History of America's Future* (New York, William Morrow, 1991).
2. See Rossel, Pierre, Miller, Riel and Jorgensen, Ulrik (eds), 'Weak Signals', Special issue, *Futures*, 44 (2), 195–276, April 2012.
3. Cole, Sam, 'Global issues and futures: a theory and pedagogy for heuristic modelling', *Futures*, 40 (9), 777–87, 2008.

Chapter 6
1. Kahn and Wiener, *The Year 2000*, *op cit*.
2. Godet, Michel, *Creating Futures: Scenario Planning as a Strategic Management Tool* (Paris: Economica, 2001), p. 18.
3. *Ibid.*, p. 62.
4. Wright, George and Cairns, George, *Scenario Thinking: Practical Approaches to the Future* (London: Palgrave Macmillan, 2011), pp. 28–45.

Chapter 7
1. Dreborg, K.H., 'Essence of backcasting', *Futures*, 28 (9), 813–28, 1996.
2. Dortmans, Peter J., 'Forecasting, backcasting, migration landscapes and strategic planning maps', *Futures*, 37 (4) 273–85, May 2005.
3. See http://www.goteborg2050.se/english.htm.
4. I am grateful to Wendy Schultz for pointing this out.
5. Boulding, Elise, 'Women's visions of the future', in Masini, Eleonora (ed.), *Visions of desirable societies* (London: Pergamon, 1983).
6. Henderson, Hazel, *Building a win-win world: Life beyond global economic warfare* (San Francisco: Berret-Koehler, 1996).

7. Joshi, Nandini, 'Women can change the future', *Futures*, 24 (9), 931–7, November 1992.
8. Inyatullah, Sohail, *Questioning the Future* (Taipei: Tamkang University, 2002), p. 218.

Chapter 8
1. Voros, Joseph, 'Integral futures: an approach to futures inquiry', *Futures*, 40 (2), 190–201, March 2008.
2. Slaughter, Richard A., 'What difference does "integral" make?', *Futures*, 40 (2), 120–37, March 2008.
3. For a more detailed discussion see Sardar, Ziauddin, *Orientalism* (Buckingham: Open University Press, 1999).
4. Inayatullah, Sohail, 'Causal layered analysis: an integrative and transformative theory and method', in Glenn, Jerome and Gordon, Theodore (eds), *Futures Research Methodology* (Washington D.C.: The Millennium Project, 2009), version 3.0.

Chapter 9
1. Nandy, Ashis, *Traditions, Tyranny and Utopias* (Delhi: Oxford University Press, 1987), pp. 6–13.
2. Kumar, Krishan, *Utopianism* (Buckingham: Open University Press, 1991).
3. Al-Farabi, *'On the Perfect State'*, trans. by Richard Walzar, *Great Books of the Islamic World* (Cambridge: Kazi Publishing, 1997).
4. See Tufayl, Ibn, 'The Story of Hayy ibn Yaqzān' (1169–79) in *Two Andalusian Philosophers*, trans. by Jim Colville (London: Kegan Paul International, 1999); or download Simon Ockley's 1708 translation of *Hayy ibn Yaqzan* from http://www.muslimphilosophy.com/books/hayy.pdf.
5. Unfortunately, it only exists in manuscript form.
6. Mahfouz, Naguib, *The Journey of Ibn Fattouma* (New York: Anchor Books, 1993).
7. Bloch, Ernst, *The Principle of Hope* (Cambridge, MA: MIT Press, 1995).
8. van der Helm, Ruud, 'The vision phenomenon: towards a theoretical underpinning of visions of the future and the process of envisioning', *Futures*, 41 (2), 96–104, March 2009.
9. Suvin, Darko, 'On the poetics of the science fiction genre', in Rose, Mark (ed.), *Science Fiction: Twentieth Century Views* (New York: Prentice Hall, 1972), p. 61.
10. Sardar, Ziauddin, 'Introduction', in Sardar, Ziauddin and Cubitt, Sean (eds), *Aliens R US: The Other in Science Fiction Cinema* (London: Pluto, 2002), p. 2.

11. Wells, H.G., *When the Sleeper Wakes* (London: Penguin classics, 2005).
12. Collie, Natalie, 'Cities of the imagination: science fiction, urban space, and community engagement in urban planning', *Futures*, 43 (4), 424–31, May 2011.

Chapter 10

1. Chakraborty, Arnab, 'Enhancing the role of participatory scenario planning processes: lessons from Reality Check exercises', *Futures*, 43 (4), 387–99, May 2011.
2. Stevenson, Tony, 'Courage and resilience: creating Filipino futures', *Futures*, 39 (4), 463–74, May 2007.
3. Leicester, Graham, 'Sustaining human aspirations: action learning in Falkirk', *Journal of Futures Studies*, 10 (1), 123–4, August 2005.
4. Teske, Kate, 'Futures in government: use of anticipatory action learning to explore public service futures', *Journal of Futures Studies*, 10 (1), 119–22, August 2005.
5. Gould, Steve, 'Maroochy 2025 Community Visioning and Action – A Case Study of Anticipatory Action Learning Practices in Use Within Maroochy Shire, Queensland, Australia', *Journal of Futures Studies*, 10 (1), 125–32, August 2005.

Chapter 11

1. *Scientific American*, September 2010, pp. 74–9.
2. Kaempffert, Waldemar, 'Miracles you'll see in the next fifty years', Modern Mechanix, available at: http://blog.modernmechanix.com/miracles-youll-see-in-the-next-fifty-years/.
   http://blog.modernmechanix.com/miracles-youll-see-in-the-next-fifty-years/.
3. See Sardar, Ziauddin (ed.), 'The Morning After', Special issue, *Futures*, 32 (1), January–February 2000.
4. Tonn, Bruce E., 'Ensuring the future', Special issue, *Futures*, 32 (1), 17–26, January–February 2000.

Index

About the author

Ziauddin Sardar, writer, broadcaster, cultural critic and futurist, is Professor of Law and Society at Middlesex University. He was editor of *Futures*, the journal of policy, planning and futures studies, from 1999 to 2012. He is the author of over 50 books, including *The Future of Muslim Civilisation* (1979), *Islamic Futures: The Shape of Ideas to Come* (1985), *Rescuing All Our Futures* (1999) and *Islam, Postmodernism and Other Futures: A Ziauddin Sardar Reader* (2003). He has served on the Executive Board of the World Futures Studies Federation, and is widely known as a public intellectual who appears frequently on radio and television. Currently he is Consulting Editor of *Futures* and co-editor of the quarterly *Critical Muslim*.